GW00992316

THE LIFE & TIMES OF LUANG PHAW WAT PAKNAM

DHAMMAKĀYA FOUNDATION
PATUM THANI, THAILAND

from the same distributors

Academic

9789748920931	Buddhism into the Year 2000
9789748235875	Palitext CDROM Database of the Entire Pali Canon

Biography

9789748940946	The Life & Times of Luang Phaw Wat Paknam
9789749274668	Second to None: Khun Yay Chandra Khon·nok·yoong

Childrens'

9789748237954	Lion & a Woodpecker
9789748237985	The Malicious Fox
9789748237961	Matuposaka Jataka
9789749162033	Buddha's Life
9789745195264	Values Education for Peace: Peace Ethics for Kids
9789744990914	Values Education for Peace: Peace Ethics for Youth
9789746435932	The Lord Buddha's History

Scripture-Based Exegesis

9789749058732	Buddha's First Teaching
9789749095218	Vanijja Sutta
9789749058718	Fruits of True Monkhood
9789749099612	Reforming Society means Reforming Human Nature
9789748277707	Man's Personal Transformation
9789749313558	Manual of Peace
9789749423035	Visudhivaca Vol.1
9789743498152	Visudhivaca Vol.2
9789748761824	Blueprint for a Global Being

Lifestyle, Meditation, Inspirational

9789749498415	Living in Peace without Worry
9789748785547	Start Meditation Today!
9789749360781	How to raise the children to be Good People
9789740938002	Pages to Happiness
9789810577575	Tomorrow the world will change
9789749498408	Right Understanding (Optimistic Wisdom)
9789740973768	Warm Hearted Family
9789749478301	Pearls of Inner Wisdom (pocket)
9789810585211	Pearls of Inner Wisdom
9789810596378	Journey to Joy
9789810800444	Lovely Love
9789745193109	Family Day by Day
9786167200095	The Middle Way Once More

Foreign Language

9789749180914	De levensgeschiedenis van Luang Pou Wat Paknam (NL)
9782953405615	La vie et l'oeuvre de Luang Pou Wat Paknam (FR)

Instructional

9789749229330	The Ordination
9789749455371	Little Book of Buddhist Chanting
9786167200071	Little Book of Buddhist Chanting (London Edition)

Commemorative

9789749297414	Sharing is Great: Tsunami

This book is dedicated to
Kuhn Yay Maha Ratana
Upasika Chandra Kohn.nok.yoong
through whose example
we can appreciate
the profundity of the teachings of
Luang Phaw Wat Paknam Bhasicharoen

A Dhammakaya Foundation paperback
First edition 1996
Second revised edition 1998
Thirrd revised edition 2003
Fourth revised edition 2010

Published by the Dhammakaya Foundation
Department of International Relations
Khlong Luang, Patum Thani 12120
Thailand

National Library of Thailand Cataloging in Publication Data

Dhammakaya Foundation.
The Life & Times of Luang Phaw Wat Paknam
Bangkok: Dhammakaya Foundation, 1996.
166p.
1. Phra Mongkol-Thepmuni (Sod Chanthasaro) 1886-1959
I. Title
294.30922

ISBN 978 974 89409 4 6

Printed and bound in Thailand by
SMK Printing Co. Ltd., 5/1 Soi Wannawan 2, 14 Charoen Nakorn Road, Klongtasai, Klongsarn, Bangkok 10600. Tel. +66-2-4389972 to 3, 8620133 to 4. Fax +66-2-4395405.
smkprinting@smkprinting.com

Contents

Prologue

Siam before the turn of the century was a green and luxuriant land — a land of paddy fields with sparkling waterways chock-a-block with heaving river barges laden with rice destined for the royal capital. Society was at peace — the people gentle, forgiving and inextricably rooted in the Buddhist heritage that had been a pillar of Siamese society since the thirteenth century. At that time, Siam was materially poor. People dressed modestly, even trousers being considered an extravagance. The material simplicity of life prevented the basic virtues of life from being obscured. In Siam, the social order was based on the home, with the bonds of filial warmth and duty between father and son, mother and daughter, brother and sister, closer than any colleague's or friend's. The home was the hub of society. In other countries, the roads came first and the houses would be built along the roads — but not Siam — the houses came first and the roads were built to suit the location of the houses.

In other countries people were born with rights but in Siamese society, where the emphasis was so much on accruing as many virtues as possible during the short period of one's life, people were born with duties to fulfil. A boy was not a boy but rather a son to his father, a pupil to his teacher, an older brother to the rest of his siblings. Individually, he was insignificant — he existed *only* as part of his family and *only* by fulfilling his duties to all his forms of social bond could he make an important contribution to society.

Understanding the perspective of Buddhist society as a training ground for the virtue of those in society, the temple can be seen as the centre or hub of training in each community. Even at the turn of the century, the temple was still the centre of all community activities. It was the only place to study when state schools still did not exist. The teaching was performed by the monks and moral fibre was woven into the weft of knowledge inculcated in all children. The monks were the most literate, usually being able to read Khmer and Thai script and able to translate freely for sermons to the general public (who were mostly unable to read the Buddhist scriptures for themselves). In fact, the only qualifications in the olden days were the examinations taken in Buddhist scripture.

Even the pace of life in the kingdom was set by the drum and gong in the temple precincts — the eleven o'clock drum signalling the monk's midday mealtime being the only time of day strictly observed by the Siamese people.

Temples were always maintained as a sanctuary for wildlife, and subsistence hunting and fishing which is an implicit part of Siamese culture was prohibited on the temple precinct.

Temples were of two sorts — the town temple and the forest temple. The former was the hub of the lay community. The monks had many commitments to the lay community which they had to honour, principally teaching. Town monks were always in the public eye, and instead of being enticed by the temptations of the outside world, often found themselves forced to be stricter than their fellow monks in the forest who had considerably more insulation from the high expectations of their supporters. Interaction with other people and the commitment to teach was the touchstone for self-improvement used by the town monks. Forest monks, on the other hand, used nature as the touchstone for self-improvement. The majority of monks in Siam were town monks even though, during Luang Phaw Wat Paknam's life, support for the monks in town had become sporadic. Usually, the monks in the provinces and the forests were better provided for than their fellow monks in the town. Town monks, however, had more opportunities to further their monastic education and receive monastic recognition through titles.

Monastic education had been standardized towards the 'Pahrean' system since the Siamese capital was moved to Bangkok in the reign of H.M. King Rama I (Phraputha·yodfa·chulalok, 1782-1809). The curriculum from the Ayuddhaya period was retained to form a curriculum and examination system in which monks would practise translation of Vinaya, Suttanta and the Ultimate Realities [*paramattha*], taking examinations until reaching the highest of three levels of advancement.

In the reign of H.M. King Rama II (Phrabuddha·lertla·naphalai, 1809-1824), the Supreme Patriarch revised the educational system to create a nine-tiered[1] examination system with examinations held every year.

---

1. The number nine was chosen either because the Teachings of the Buddha in the Tipitaka are of nine different styles or because the supramundance attainments comprise nine different paths and fruits.

In the reign of H.M. King Rama III (Phra Nang Klao, 1824-1851), the examinees had to undergo an oral examination testing their proficiency in translating the Pali palm-leaf scriptures into Thai. To pass no more than two mistakes were allowed. The test passage was picked at random by the Supreme Patriarch, thus each candidate received a different passage. After receiving the passage, the candidate was given a little time to read it and overcome his nervousness before entering the examination room. He would then have to translate the palm leaves in front of the board of examiners. Originally a candidate at any level had to translate three palm leaves (one leaf equalling ten lines of script) making no more than two mistakes. Later on, however, the number of leaves to be translated was reduced to two leaves in general and one for Grade IX. This type of examination was directly applicable to the traditional way of giving sermons: translating and expanding upon a chosen palm-leaf scripture in front of an assembled congregation.

Monastic study became more institutionalized in the reign of H.M. King Rama V (Chulalongkorn, 1868-1910) with the building of Mahamongkut Academy (1893) and Mahachulalongkorn Academy (1911) specifically for monks studying Pali. The written system of 'Pahrean Studies' favoured by King Chulalongkorn and the reformed Dhammayutthika sect was introduced on a small scale at Mahamongkut Academy from 1894-1900, but did not gain favour with the majority of the *Mahānikāya* monks who favoured the oral examinations held at the Grand Palace chapel. It was not until the reign of H.M. King Rama VI (Mahavajiravudh, 1910-1925) that the Prince Patriarch Vajirañana replaced the oral examination system with standardized written examinations, during the time when Luang Phaw Wat Paknam was a Pali student at Wat Phra Chetupon. Thenceforth, the emphasis on expansion of Pali meaning from the root meaning (*mūlakaccāyana*), in the Burmese style, was replaced by the memorization of the concise Pali grammar written by Prince Vajirañana himself.

The increasing number of graduates from the new educational system allowed the influence of the Sangha hierarchy instituted by the 1902 Sangha Law to spread throughout the kingdom until every monastery was connected by lines of government to the Council of Elders. Honorific and administrative titles started to proliferate in the monastic order. Such honours might seem alien to the way of life as an ascetic — however, it was nearly impossible to be a pillar of Buddhism without rank because monastic rank and seniority meant the power to act and effect change. On the lower rungs of the monastic hierarchy titles such as 'Phra Kru' denoted influence in local monastic government. On the higher levels the titles were bestowed by the king himself and any monk receiving such titles effectively gained the ability to enlarge his influence beyond his own small temple, reaching out to affect society at large and ultimately the state of Buddhism in the nation. Monastic titles meant much more than fame for any particular monk, although sometimes misunderstandings occurred.

The tradition of meditation in Thailand is as old as Buddhism in Thailand itself. During the time of Luang Phaw Wat Paknam, there were several ancient texts of meditation written in Thai along with contemporary masters who could explicate them. All of the meditation techniques available at the time had their shortfalls. They were limited in their results — often deviating in search of the miraculous rather than leading to the wisdom known by the Buddha. Elements of the *Dhammakāya* meditation technique rediscovered by Luang Phaw Wat Paknam were present in some of the contemporary meditation techniques of the time, but none of these allowed *samatha*[1] to develop naturally into *vipassanā*[2] without the need for conceptualization.

When Luang Phaw Wat Paknam was born in 1885, having attained the rarity of a human birth, he resolved with exceptional fortitude to dedicate his life to meditation and the renaissance of Buddhism in Thailand. In the verses,

Tamo tamaparāyano,
Tamo jotiparāyano
Joti tamaparāyano,
Joti jotiparāyano[3]

the Lord Buddha identified four different types of life path for people born in our world. Some people were born out of darkness into darkness. The darkness refers to the residue of evil deeds in peoples' past lives, that they could escape only after many hundreds of thousands of lifetimes in the fires of hell. When born in the human realm, they wasted their opportunity as a human, doing no further good deeds and were eventually reborn back

---

1. for definition see p.147
2. for definition see p.148
3. Tama Sutta A.ii.85

into the hell from whence they came.

Some emerged from darkness into the light. They used their human life as a turning point for their unskilful past, doing only good deeds, making only progress between heaven and the human realm from that life time onwards.

Some descended from light onto darkness — like the majority of people they wasted their chance as a human and simply took advantage of their strength and intellect to exploit those around themselves — the bad karma they amassed for themselves would drag them down into the netherland of bad rebirth for hundreds of thousands of lifetimes.

However, those few who understood the working of the cycle of existence were born out of the light and passed away into light. At the crossroads of destiny represented by the human realm, they used the power of the good deeds they had accumulated over the course of many lifetimes to progress closer to Nirvana — never more to stray outside the two worlds, heaven and the human realm. Such was the life of Luang Phaw Wat Paknam Bhasicharoen whose life never wavered from the pursuit of perfection.

Right from birth, no-one can be separated from their purpose in life. When anyone is born, sooner or later they have to ask themselves,"Why have I been born?"

Some people glibly conclude that they had simply been born to raise a family and earn a comfortable living — to have as many children as possible to shoulder the family's inheritance. Some are less than scrupulous in amassing wealth — not always earning income by honest means. They revolve in social circles that avoided visiting the temple. Usually by the time they set foot in the temple, it was already too late — all too often they were carried into the temple feet-first on a pall ready for the cremation!

Some considered their welfare both in this lifetime and the next. They accumulated wealth both for the benefit of themselves and their families and also for the benefit of the monastic community. They visited the temple, kept the basic Buddhist Precepts and practised meditation as taught by the monks of the temple. They entered the monkhood for the duration of a rainy season (three months) as part of their maturation process in order to show gratitude to their parents for giving them life and bringing them up. Some practised good deeds for only part of their lives — some for part of their youth, entering the temple to serve the monks and study Buddhism. Some practised good deeds only in middle age and indulged their childhood and old age with eating, sleeping and making merry. Others came to the temple only when awakened to the value of life by old age and sickness — but by this time they could offer little to the religion — they had come to lean on the religion rather than the religion leaning on them.

There were, however, a rare few born with a vocation to search for an end to all defilements, who resolved that the present lifetime will be their last. These were the few devoted men and women who enter the temple at an early age, not distracted by family life but who sacrificed their lives for Buddhism and trained themselves in the tradition of the Buddha all their lives. Among these select few are those monks in Thailand who ordained for life as opposed to taking temporary ordination. Such a monk was Luang Phaw Wat Paknam.

1
A Chicken's Life

> *"Born in search of gems — but when you find them, disburse them! Craving cheats us, falsity deludes us and ensnares our roiling, tortured mind — put an end to craving, escape falsity, remove yourself from sensuality, follow the threefold khanda without let, complete the sixteen tasks: until invulnerable to hardship — that you can call Nirvana if you like..."*
>
> *(Phramonkolthepmuni)*

A full-moon night of September 1916. The moon's bright face is suspended motionless against a backdrop of twinkling stars. The mirror surface of a nearby waterway is gently stirred by the night breeze and the ripples catch the light of the moon as they move towards the canal bank. It is early evening on the outskirts of Bangkok. The rain has just stopped. The raindrops still hang pendent on the leaves like jewelled tears twinkling in the moonlight.

Everything is quiet inside the main compound of Wat Bangkuvieng, except for the rasping of crickets and the chirping of insects. From outside the temple compound, the sound is carried on the breeze together with the warm smell of the dampened soil. A beam of moonlight shines through the window of the largest building illuminating a gigantic statue of the Buddha in deep meditation.

A single monk in front of the image of the Buddha is sitting equally statue-like, motionless in meditation. Although he has been sitting for a long time, his body remains erect. The moon moves across the zenith of the heavens, becoming ever brighter. The monk, clad in yellow robes is in his early thirties. His forehead shows determination, intelligence and an uncommon strength of character. A draught blowing across the hall catches the corner of his robe. At this point the monk releases a heavy breath, audible throughout the building. A half-smile appears on his face as he beams with delight. He murmurs to himself:

> "Ah! . . . it is so hard like this. This is why no one else could manage to achieve it. Sensation, memory, thought and cognition: all these must be united into one single spot. Once the mind is still, it ceases to be. Once it ceases to be, the new one can arise."

The murmur died away as suddenly as it had come. Delight is the enemy of success in meditation. He was well aware of this. Even so, for this monk with over a decade's experience, it was very hard to contain the ecstasy of fulfillment. He closed his eyes again in silence. Without rest, again and again that evening, he relived his revelation, reflecting backwards and forwards, backwards and forwards. The experience this day was the culmination of eleven years devotion and meditation.

*

Many great spiritual people are born in poverty in remote villages. Nature fastens a harmony with the cosmos, and leads them to the ultimate questions of existence.

On Friday tenth of October 1885, in the village of Songpinong, Supanburi province, Thailand, Sodh Mikaewnoi, was just another bundle of helpless humanity issuing into the world.[1] His birth differed from that of other children in only one way — at his birth, Sodh Mikaewnoi did not cry. Not even a whimper was to pass his lips, because he had been born to dry the tears of humanity.

The family house was in the north of the Songpinong commune. The house was located on a curious piece of land, the shape of a lotus leaf, surrounded by water on all sides. There had never been any outbreak of fire on this curious islet. The house was positioned to the south of the Songpinong temple on the opposite side of the canal. The temple was to the northeast of the commune, the house to the southwest.

His father was called Ngeun and his mother Sutjai. His family was renowned in the area served by Songpinong Canal because of rice trading in the district. The family had two river barges and several crew members. They shipped rice between Songpinong and the Bangkok mills or Nakorn Chaisri two or three times a month. The Mikaewnois' reputation was paramount for their success in business. The rice dealer in Songpinong would trust the Mikaewnois with the rice on credit, content to wait for the payment when they returned.

Sodh Mikaewnoi was the second born of five brothers and sisters with an older sister Dha, and three younger brothers, Sai, Phook and Samruam in order of birth.

Dha recalled from early childhood that Sodh Mikaewnoi was a smart child. When Luang Phaw Wat Paknam was still an infant, he was always highly alert and comprehending of his surroundings.

---

1. Reproduced with permission from Magness, T. (1964) *The Life and Teaching of the Venerable Chao Khun Mongkol-Thepmuni, the late abbot of Wat Paknam Bhasicharoen* (Bangkok: Groarke). p.1

One day he wanted to know find out about the origin of lying. When the nursemaid took him on her hip and carried him outside beyond the eaves of the house, the infant raised his head and pointed at the moon while at the same time cooing,"Err, err."

The maid saw the infant's gesture and understood that the baby was crying for the moon and teased,"Oh! Oh! You want the moon, do you? — just a moment I'll just bring it down!"

The baby heard the maid's response and knew in a flash that this is what a lie is like — saying something even when you know that there is no way you can fulfil your promise.

It was the habit of affectionate female relatives to pick up babies and rub cheeks with them. Maybe it was the influence of many previous lifetimes as a monk, but in any case, even as a child, Sodh disliked being picked up by the womenfolk. He had a way of expressing his dislike of being handled. Every time he was picked up, Sodh would grab the corner of his caretaker's blouse and refuse to let go until he was put down again. To begin with, the child's protest took the caretakers by surprise. There were many a red-faced caretaker holding the infant up to their cheek only to find themselves bared to the midriff! The caretakers gradually became more cautious about handling the child.

Another time, when he was a year old, Sodh started to cry for some cakes, asking for his mother. The relative who was looking after him, tried to comfort him by saying that his mother had gone to work in the fields. At this he suddenly stopped crying. His mother, he thought, had to go to work in the fields. This meant only one thing — he had been born into a poor family. From that day forth he never again cried for cakes.[1]

---

1. from *ibid*. p.1

As he grew up he showed himself to be a very determined child — whenever he had set his heart on achieving something, he would always persevere until achieving success. He used to help his mother tend the oxen, and disregarding his age and size, would always plunge fearlessly into a neighbour's herd in order to retrieve missing oxen, no matter where they might have strayed. It often took him until dark before he ended his quest, leading the oxen back through the night. He wouldn't dare return empty-handed. When he had managed to track down his charge, he would return triumphant upon the back of the buffalo — singing as he steered the buffalo home.

Not only responsibility but also compassion was an innate part of Sodh Mikaewnoi's character. Another of his chores was to help his parents plough the fields each morning. As it neared eleven o'clock, he would gaze up to check the position of the sun to note what time it was. The new generation was not so assiduous in looking after its beasts. His sister often took him to task for this, accusing him of only waiting for the moment to take time off. However, the old folks knew that this was not in his mind, but rather the old proverb that 'eleven kills the buffaloes'.[1] For him and the older generation it was a thoughtless cruelty for one's beast still to be ploughing when the eleven o'clock drum was struck. He kept to his principles no matter what anyone might have said. If he saw that the oxen had been overworked and had become tired, he would lead them off for a bath before letting them loose to graze.

As he matured, he began to travel with his father and

---

1. from *ibid*. p.1-2

help row the barge. In such a way, he helped the old folks until the age of nine.

One day, the barge passed a waterside spirit house of the sort common throughout the country. This particular shrine was widely rumoured to be sacred and anybody who passed by felt compelled to make an offering or at least pay their respects. Sodh thought to himself that the calvary had nothing to do with the Buddha, or the Dhamma or the Sangha. It had nothing to do with any part of the Triple Gem. "Why do people feel so compelled to pay respect to this shrine?" he thought. "Whatever the others may say, I will surely not be among those to pay respect at this shrine."

Such discriminative thought is uncommon in most children — and in the case of Sodh Mikaewnoi it is interesting to note that he was so stalwart in his belief even before he came to know the real meaning of the 'Triple Gem'.[1]

When Sodh was nine he had the chance to start his formal education after his uncle became a *bhikkhu*. Sodh's mother sent him across the canal to study with his uncle at the village temple of Wat Songpinong. In those days, before the establishment of state schools, *bhikkhus* were the only teachers. It was customary for a *bhikkhu* not to take residence in one place for too long. Thus, after only a few months, his uncle moved to another temple, and he followed. The *bhikkhu* next moved to a temple in Thonburi, across the river from Bangkok. As this was quite a distance from his native village, the young boy did not follow him. Instead he was despatched to Bang Pla Temple, in Banglain, Nakorn Pathom[2] (hometown of his father's side of the family) where he assiduously studied Thai and Khom,

---

1. see definition p.148 2. from *ibid*. p.2

under the guidance of Phra Acharn Sap.

Luang Phaw was a true auto-didact, and never needed prodding from anyone. Such ability is not a skill developed in a single lifetime but is the fruit of many lifetime's pursuit of wisdom, many lifetimes accruing the merit that purifies the mind. This same gift subsequently enabled him to discover *Vijjā Dhammakāya,* lost for so many thousands of years, without any instruction or instructor and *mirabile dictu,* to instruct and initiate others in *Vijjā Dhammakāya*!

Sodh was fourteen when his father died. As soon as the news reached him in Banglain, he returned to Songpinong. As the eldest son, the burden of running the family business and supporting his mother and family fell on his young shoulders — however, with Sodh's wisdom, judgment and leadership, he soon won the love and respect of his relatives and crew.

Once, when the boat was anchored in Bangkok, his brother-in-law's employee stole a thousand baht. He went to the police and together they pursued the thief by boat all night until dawn. Sodh spied the thief at one of the windows of a house and the officer was informed — but before the boat could come to shore the thief hid himself. Noticing that the man had left a trail of wet footprints, Sodh told the police to wait out front while he tracked the thief himself. He found the man hiding behind the haystacks. As soon as he saw Sodh, the thief dived into the straw. The police had already been informed; he was pulled out and handcuffed. They managed to retrieve every last baht.[1]

Sodh was always keen on developing himself — never content with his own level of development. He would emulate the success of others, and incorporate their

1. from *ibid*. p.2-3

virtuous characteristics. If the success among any of his relatives or companions exceeded his, he would extend heartfelt congratulations to that person and see how he could learn from that person's success. Envy was alien to Sodh's way of thinking. On the contrary, if anyone fell on hard times, he would describe their lifestyle as a 'chicken's life,' and try to advise them of a better way to lead their life. Sodh's earnestness brought him fortune. His business grew and finances prospered.

The sands of fortune, however, were to shift one day when Sodh, aged eighteen, together with his earnings from a cargo of rice, was rowing two empty barges back upstream. The river banks were infested with pirates and rapids. When the river was in full spate barges had to detour through the most notorious pirate-ridden canal, Bang Ee-Taen, a narrow stretch of canal dreaded by boatmen. The curse, 'Rapid water — narrow creek — that's where the worst of bandits make their lair,' tells it all. Only a few lucky boats managed to pass Bang Ee-Taen without being robbed. Usually they would travel in a convoy for security. That day Sodh's boat was the only boat in sight. As he turned into the creek, the first intimations stirred. The fear of death flickered before his eyes. Sodh ordered his crewmen to switch position — manning the tiller on the stern of the barge. Sodh knew the strategy of the pirates. They would attack either the captain or the helmsman first. If he hid himself beneath the prow — he might double his chances of surviving an attack.

Sodh had a rifle. He grabbed it and strode towards the bow as the boat gradually glided into a remote part of the canal. He took the oars but was wracked with guilt:

> "All the crew gets from me for looking after this wretched barge is ten or eleven baht a month. Why should I let them be the first to die when I'm the one who owns it? If disaster strikes, they should look after their own skins because they have wives and children dependent on them for the rice in their bellies."

He called the crewmen back to the oars and sat at the tiller with the rifle in his lap. By that time, however, the boat had drifted on and was approaching the mouth of the canal, where many cargo vessels were anchored waiting to traverse the lock as soon as the waters rose. The vessels were so congested that none could make headway, and the merchants were shouting among themselves. The danger of being attacked had passed.[1]

Although he had passed through the crisis safely, the whole episode left him with a deep sorrow for his fellow men — to go through such an ordeal just to avail themselves of a day's wages:

> "Didn't my own father ply the same river with the same wares and the same dangers until the end of his days? Didn't he become fatally ill on just such a voyage? Am I to learn nothing more from life than he did? Does no-one have spare time from the scurry for a livelihood — to rest and be thankful? Does society so despise the unmade man to ostracize him until he can earn himself riches? Material wealth is so ingrained in our values that we don't know a beginning or an end of it. Those who initiated material values are long-since dead — and how much better are they for their values in the grave? All are dead. Dead is my father. Dead will I be too in the none-too-distant future..."

---

1. from *ibid*. p.3-4

2
Ordination

> *"The majority of human beings have their eyes closed — they are still asleep. If human beings could attain **Dhammakāya**, they would be awake. But without attaining **Dhammakāya** and becoming one with **Dhammakāya**, they are doomed to slumber forever."* (*Phramonkolthepmuni*)

Brooding in the aftermath of his escape, his blood ran cold. He felt so moved that he lay down in the stern and made believe he was dead — that his disembodied spirit was wandering about seeking for his dead forbears and those friends he had loved. But they ignored him because they couldn't see him — he was only a spirit. He threw clods of earth and sticks at them — but they mistook him for a ghost from the forest because they couldn't see the perpetrator. Drifting on in his quest for this person or that, no-one could see him or would take any interest.[1] The spectre of unavoidable death forced him to examine the possibilities available to him:

> "Here I am. I don't even know if I'll be alive to see tomorrow's sunrise — and still I'm scurrying like the rest of them for evanescent riches. On my deathbed, even the closest of relatives, the closest of friends, can but look on helplessly. Only I alone can further my own destiny."

1.from *ibid*. p.4

He lit three sticks of incense, pressed them between the palms of his hands and made the following resolution with heartfelt determination:

> "Don't let me die now! At least let me die in the yellow robe. If only I can ordain — I will remain in the monkhood until my days are done!"

That day he escaped danger unscathed, but the vow he made was never to leave his mind. At first he kept his ambitions to himself.[1] Later he began to discuss his plans with others. He planned to ordain but could not shrug off his responsibility to support the family. He needed to leave them enough savings to support themselves in his absence and calculated the rate of inflation from the surest indicator — the rise in the price of bananas. He set to work with a fervour in order to accumulate without delay, sufficient wealth for his mother to support herself and the family for the rest of their lives. Six months later, in May 1903, he loaded rice sacks onto his barges for the last time. He told the crew to make the trip to Bangkok on his behalf. He gave the most trusted of his crewmen the consummate authority to manage the rice deal.

Sodh turned from the wharf a free man and entered Wat Songpinong as a postulant or '*nag*.' He studied with Phrapalad 'Yang,' the abbot of the temple, preparing himself for ordination. Sodh diligently studied the verses of ordination and the abbreviated monk's discipline. In July 1903, along with seven others, Sodh was ordained at Wat Songpinong and was given

---

1. We know of his intentions only because his thoughts were written down and found among his autobiographical papers.

the monk's name 'Candasaro Bhikkhu'. The name 'Candasaro' was in the traditional Pali language and meant "the one with a bright radiance like the moon". As the ordination ceremony approached, someone was sent to invite Phra Acharn 'Dee' of Wat Pratusarn, Suphanburi to be Candasaro's Preceptor. Phra Kru Vinyananuyok (Nieng Indajoto) was *kammavācācāriya*[1] and Phra Acharn 'Nong' Indasuvaṇṇo was *anusāvanācāriya*.[2] Both the *kammavācācāriya* and *anusāvanācāriya* were resident at Wat Songpinong.

Candasaro Bhikkhu began his studies the day after his ordination. He began to study the Pali scriptures. He memorized the chanting and the Patimokkha. Unlike many monks, he studied both meditation and scripture in earnest. Phra Acharn 'Nong' was his first teacher.

During his first rains-retreat (*vassa*) at the temple, he learned the Pali scriptures by heart up to '*avijjāpaccayā*'. He became curious about the meaning of this word. He asked a fellow monk who had been ordained for three *vassa*s for the translation, but received the answer:

> "Brother, we don't translate the Scriptures here, we just recite them — if you want to know more you will have to study in Bangkok..."

He returned to his room perplexed by the *bhikkhus*' lack of textual scholarship. After only seven months' ordination, Candasaro's heart was already set on furthering his studies in the capital. Even so, the Pali studies were for him only a means to an end — mastery of the knowledge of the Buddha through meditation. He concealed a

---

1. see definition p.146 2. see definition p.145

bundle of the Mahāsatipaṭṭhāna Sutta scriptures at Wat Songpinong with the intention that as soon as he was able to translate them fluently, he would discontinue his Pali studies in Bangkok and devote himself entirely to meditation.

He went to his mother for permission to proceed to the capital. She was far from enthusiastic, but he finally persuaded her. He asked her for the requisites for the trip, and resolved never to ask for such support from her again.[1]

At the end of the rains, once monks were free to travel again, Candasaro Bhikkhu left Wat Songpinong and enrolled at Wat Phra Chetupon (also known as Wat Bodhi) in Bangkok. There he continued his study of the monk's discipline (*Vinaya*).

His younger brother Phook accompanied him to Bangkok too, to study and practice Buddhism. One night, in his fourth year as a *bhikkhu*, Candasaro had a vision. A shadowy man appeared and offered him a bowl of sand. He took a pinch. When his brother was offered some, the boy took two handfuls. A few days after the vision, Candasaro fell ill suddenly and was removed to another temple for treatment. Initially, his eighteen-year old brother tended Candasaro, but before long grew seriously ill himself. Candasaro soon recovered. As soon as his illness subsided, he took his brother hurriedly back to Songpinong for treatment. The boy did not recover and died soon afterwards.[2] After the cremation Candasaro returned alone to Wat Phra Chetupon.

Moving to Wat Phra Chetupon meant Candasaro Bhikkhu had many difficulties distracting him from his studies. Sometimes there was insufficient food to feed all

---

1. from *ibid*. p.5

2. from *ibid*. p.5-6

the monks. Some days his total sustenance for the day would be a single orange. Some days he would receive no food at all. The first day Candasaro Bhikkhu went for his almsround he came back with an empty bowl. The second day was no better. He began to wonder:

> "Even when a man has sacrificed all worldly pleasure to practice the Precepts and perpetuate Buddhism — is it his lot to starve for his cause?"

Thoughts of death entered his mind again but they did not upset him. He thought:

> "At least if I starve to death through the hard-heartedness of these city-folk, I will be a martyr stirring them to pity so that the rest of my brethren might have sufficient food in the future."

On the third day he went for alms again. This time he received a ladleful of rice and a banana.[1] Weak and fatigued from two days on an empty stomach, Candasaro Bhikkhu made his weary way back to his room. That day he sat down to take his meal at the door of his room. As he was reflecting upon his food, a mangy, stray mongrel meandered into view — so emaciated that its bones seemed to show through its skin. It had obviously been starving for days. Today might be its last. Candasaro threw the remainder of his alms to the dog and made the solemn wish:

> "Through the power of this generosity in the face of such adversity, may starvation never again cross

---

1. from *ibid*. p.6

> my path. Through the purity of my Precepts and these truthful words may I never again return from almsround with an empty bowl."

Only then did he part with the meal. Although the dog was thin and had probably eaten nothing for days, it ate only the rice and left the banana untouched.

Somewhat dismayed at this, Candasaro thought of retrieving the banana, but recalled that a *bhikkhu* does not take back anything which he has already given away. It was not fitting, therefore, to do so — unless, of course, someone were to re-offer it, with both hands, as is the custom.[1] No such person, however, appeared.

From that day forth, however, through the purity of Candasaro's Precepts and his forthrightness — he was never to return with an empty bowl from his almsround — he always had more than enough food to share with his fellow brethren.

Candasaro reflected upon the difficulties he himself and his fellow brethren had experienced through lack of food. This led him to vow:

> "One day when I receive sufficient support from benefactors I will build a kitchen so that the monastic community can put all their energies into Scriptural study and meditation without having to worry where their next meal will come from."

It would take a decade before Candasaro's dream became a reality.

---

1. from *ibid*. p.6

3
Scriptural Studies

"Education can change a student's life for the better — knowledge is a king's heritage — accessible to the common man, it benefit us for life."
(Phramonkolthepmuni)

At that time the education of monks and novices began with memorizing the Suttas in their original Pali language. When these had been committed to memory, the monks would have to memorize the grammar of the Scriptures: i.e. the Pali root forms (*mūlakaccāyana*) from euphonic combination (*sandhi*) onwards. Candasaro pursued his Scriptural studies in the same way, continuing his studies with nouns (*nāma*), secondary derivation (*taddhita*), indeclinables (*ākhayāta*) and primary derivation (*kita*). Only then would the monks be allowed to begin the study of the Scriptures. Candasaro memorized the foundation materials and started studying his first scripture — the Dhammapada. When he had mastered the second part of the Dhammapada, he studied the first part.

In those days, the Scriptures were not in book form, but etched on palm leaves using Khom script. Students didn't study the Scriptures in order from 'page one' onwards but picked chapters at random, because palm-leaf scriptures are loose-leafed. Some students studying the Dhammapada started with earlier chapters, some with the later ones. As a result, the more students attending a class, the more bundles of scriptures each had to lug to class. If a student studied privately with a teacher, he need bring only his own bundles (his own chosen texts). If however a class had ten students, he would have to bring not only his own scripture-bundles, but those chosen by all his other classmates too! Students attending large classes would be bent double under the weight of scripture bundles. He went on to study two other texts popular among contemporary monks — the Maṅgaladīpanī and Sārasaṅgaha, until he became so well versed that he was able to teach others.

Academic life was by no means easy. Students had to seek out their teacher. Lessons were not held in classrooms but in the teacher's quarters. If a the teacher happened to reside in a remote temple, it was the duty of the students to wend the weary miles each day. After breakfast Candasaro would cross the river from Wat Phra Chetupon to Wat Arun (Rajavararaam). At eleven he would return to Wat Phra Chetupon for lunch. In the afternoon, he had to attend a class at Wat Mahathat. For his evening class, sometimes he would have to travel to Wat Suthat, sometimes to Wat Samphleum. By night, he had to attend the last class of the day at his home temple, Wat Phra Chetupon. However, it was not every day of the week that he had such a busy schedule.

No matter how far away the lessons were, how heavy the scriptures or how tired he felt, Candasaro was never absent from his classes. With his scriptures on his shoulder, he was such a frequent passenger on the Chaophraya River ferry between Peacock Gate Jetty and Wat Arun, that even the jetty-keeper realized his academic perseverance. His perseverance also stirred many of the regular passengers to faith. Many invited him to receive their alms each morning. Others offered to pay his living expenses. The most faithful of his sponsors was the pedlar named 'Nuam' who undertook to provide Candasaro with breakfast and lunch daily.

For years Candasaro travelled to various schools to study the Scriptures. More and more people were inspired by his diligence and tried to find ways to help him. The monks' food improved greatly. So strong was the support that Candasaro succeeded in establishing a private Pali college at Wat Phra Chetupon using his own quarters as a classroom. He invited Phramahapee Vasuttamo, a talented monk of Pali Grade V who had followed the abbot, Somdej Phraputhacharn (Khem Dhammasaro), from Wat Mahathat, Nakorn Pathom as a permanent lecturer. Candasaro catered for as many as ten students and teachers in the school at his own expense, and taught Pali up to Grade V.

Times, however, were changing in the world of Thai monastic education. The Council of Elders issued a policy directive to base Pali study on grammar (rather than free translation from the root meaning). Wat Phra Chetupon was therefore left with no choice but to merge its various private colleges into one, in order to toe the line. Accordingly, Candasaro's Pali School ceased to exist. Candasaro Bhikkhu was unperturbed however by the curriculum changes. Even though Pali examinations changed from oral to written — he persevered to adapt and was an inspiration to others.

Even though Candasaro Bhikkhu seemed to devote himself to the study of the Scriptures, he always made time for meditation as well. In those days he followed the technique taught by his *anusāvanācāriya*, Phra Acharn Nong. On the quarter-moon days, when he was free from Scriptural study, he travelled to different temples renowned for their meditation teachers.

He studied with Phrasangavaranuwongse (Phra Acharn Eam) of Wat Rajasiddharam, Bangkok; Phra Kru Nyanavirat (Po) of Wat Phra Chetupon, Bangkok; Phra Acharn Singh, Wat Lakorn Thaam (behind Wat Rakhangkositaram), Thonburi; Phramonkolthipmuni (Muy) the abbot of Wat Chakrawat, Bangkok, and; Phra Acharn Pleum of Wat Kao Yai, Thamaka district, Kanchanaburi. All these famous masters were regarded as the foremost of their time in Buddhist meditation. As a result of their level of discipline, all had multitudinous students. Candasaro completed the teachings of all these masters within an exceptionally short period of time.

"Venerable sir, is there anything else I should know?" This question was frequently raised by Candasaro at the end of his masters' discourses.

All too often the master would answer, "I cannot teach you anything further. You are now my equal. Come and teach alongside me!" Phra Kru Nyanavirat and Phra Acharn Singh both testified to Candasaro's attainment and elected him to teach. Candasaro was dissatisfied however, with his own level of knowledge. He thought, "My knowledge is too superficial to qualify me as a meditation master."

He humbly refused to teach anyone. He left his old teachers to travel alone, searching for more knowledge — going anywhere in Thailand where there was a reputable master.

Amongst his meditation experiences, at Wat Rajasiddharam,[1] Candasaro managed to perceive a bright and lucent sphere, the size of the yolk of an egg, right in the centre of his diaphragm[2] — demonstrating that elements of the path of practice he was later to pursue and develop were still present in fragmentary form in the meditation tradition of ancient Siam.

His travels took him to his old temple of Wat Songpinong. In those days the elder monks never paid much attention to study. The younger monks who were interested in studying, without any help from the elders, didn't know where to begin. Usually those interested in studying would be sent to Bangkok. Thus when Candasaro went to stay at Wat Songpinong in his eleventh year of monkhood he was the prime mover in establishing a school, in spite of many obstacles — a school which still exists today under the foundation he set up.

While Candasaro was at Wat Songpinong he recalled the bundle of Mahāsatipaṭṭhāna Sutta scriptures he had concealed since his ordination. He realized, in his eleventh year of monkhood, that he had reached the benchmark he had set for himself in Pali studies. He was now able to translate that bundle fluently — and in accordance with his original intention, would discontinue his Pali studies and undertake the task of studying meditation in earnest...

---

1. from Newell, C.S. (2008) *Monks, meditation and missing links: continuity, "orthodoxy" and the vijjā dhammakāya in Thai Buddhism*, PhD. Diss. (SOAS, Univ. of London). p.260

2. from Magness *ibid*. p.8

4
Early Studies in Meditation

> *"Stopping the mind is the essence — it is both the path and the fruit of Nirvana. Even those who practise charity and keep the Precepts are not as close to Nirvana as those whose mind is at a standstill."*
>
> *(Phramonkolthepmuni)*

It was only in retrospect that Candasaro realized that if he had continued to study and attained a high degree of scholarship, the Sangha authorities would surely have recruited him to work in an academic capacity to the detriment of his meditation practice. From that time onwards Candasaro devoted himself entirely to the study of meditation.

He became a wandering *bhikkhu* and practiced '*dhutaṅga*' for self-purification, leaving the comforts of a fixed abode behind. He requested a forest umbrella (*klod*) from his aunt, under which to sleep, and refused to accept one from anyone else. He wished her to receive the merit arising from this offering, to repay his debt of gratitude to her. He left for the provinces, returned after a short period, and gave away the umbrella to another *bhikkhu*. Later he made a second trip, and again received an umbrella from his aunt.[1] Eventually, after several months of such practice, he concluded that there must be a better way to gain the Truth taught by Lord Buddha — a way presently lacking which would make meditation easier to learn and accessible to all people.

1. from *ibid*. p.8

He started to be his own master following the great Buddhist Manual, *The Path of Purity* written by Buddhaghosa, a famous Buddhist exegete of the fifth century A.D..

Once he was on *dhutaṅga* in Supan Buri and was about to set up his *klod* at a deserted temple near Wat Phrasri Ratana Mahathat when he saw children driving a herd of oxen into the area.

"Don't let the cows come one step further lest you earn yourselves a grave demerit," he warned.

"Take no notice of him," said the children. "The monk doesn't know what he's talking about — he probably wants the place to himself", they presumed.

"Don't you know that there are Buddha images under the ground here?" asked Candasaro, gesturing. "If you don't believe me, try digging at that spot."

The childrens' curiosity was aroused. They dug where he said and precisely where he had pointed found several Buddha images. The precision of the monk's knowledge gained the childrens' respect and they apologized to him for having been so presumptuous.

In fact that temple was half-ruined. There were over a hundred large and small Buddha images left in a poor state of repair by vandalism or simply old age. Some Buddha images had heads or arms missing. Candasaro felt he must try to remedy this neglect and started teaching meditation to the locals and encouraging the faithful to help with repair work by teaching the meritorious fruits of such acts. A good deal of progress was made with the repairs as the number of people increased. The large number of faithful and the single-hearted devotion to the restoration of the ruined temple was an uncommon occurrence in rural Suphan Buri. Eventually the large congregation attracted the prying eyes of the Supan Buri authorities who mistook the gathering for a nascent uprising. The district governor went to speak with the monastic governor for the area, who at that time happened to be Somdej Phra Wanarat (Pearn Tissadatto) of Wat Phra Chetupon. The authorities accused Candasaro of conduct unbefitting of a monk. They pleaded with Somdej Phra Wanarat to summon Candasaro back. News of the complaints reached Candasaro and with respect for the authorities, he dropped all that he was doing — all that he had accomplished — and moved on to Wat Songpinong, in order to avoid 'rocking the boat'.

He remembered the spacious shrine hall of Wat Phra Chetupon as suitable for meditation. Nevertheless he recalled his spiritual debt to his first scriptural teacher, Phra Acharn 'Chum', abbot of Wat Bangkuvieng, Bangkoknoi (Canal) who had imparted to him the *mūlakaccāyana* and Dhammapada text. With the wish to repay that debt, he paid his respects to Somdej Phraputhacharn (Khem Dhammasaro), the abbot of Wat Phra Chetupon and went to spend his eleventh rains-retreat at Wat Boatbon Bangkuvieng in order to share what he had learned of the scriptures with the monks and novices of that temple.

He was about to enter the 'Rains' Retreat at Wat Boatbon. Before going for alms that morning, he reflected that he had been ordained for eleven long years but still hadn't tasted the Truth found by Lord Buddha, although he had studied both meditation and Scriptures without rest during all that time. He resolved that he ought to be called a wastrel, if he didn't continue to try his utmost.

His almsround completed, he finished his daily duties before going to the main shrine hall to meditate. He resolved that if he didn't hear the midday drum which signalled lunchtime, he wouldn't break off from his meditation. Not only this, he resolved not to waver in this practice of sitting meditation, whatever suffering might disturb his single-mindedness. He resolved not to swerve from his purpose until he recognised some portion of the real Truth taught by the Buddha. He fully realised that taking such a vow might cost him his life, but acknowledged that he could not continue to be considered a worthy monk unless he could fulfil this act.

It was about eight in the morning when he started to meditate with the mantra *'Sammā-arahaṃ'*. The intense pain in his legs made him feel that the time passed extraordinary slowly. The pain increased in his body so much that he felt as if every bone was going to tear apart. The pain increased his agitation until suddenly he realised:

> "I have never felt such pain before. Why, now that I have sworn not to change my position in meditation, is the pain so much more intense than ever before? My mind has never been as agitated as this. How much longer must I endure this suffering before I hear the sound of the eleven o'clock drum?"

The more he thought, the more agitated he became. He nearly gave up many times — but because of the strength of his fighting-spirit after making such a resolution, he felt it was essential to carry on to the end, even if it cost his life. He knew that when the mind is agitated, it cannot find peace. So, he rose to a new level of tolerance and began to let go of the pain, detaching himself from the suffering. Suddenly his mind became still and firmly established at the very centre of his body. He perceived a bright clear shining sphere of Dhamma. The size of the sphere of Dhamma was equal to the yolk of an egg. The experience which filled his whole body was one of inexplicable bliss which rinsed away all the agony. At that moment he heard the sound of the eleven o'clock drum.

That morning his midday meal had a special flavour which he had never tasted before — the flavour of spiritual success. This experience in meditation which had arisen in his awareness uplifted his whole existence. He thought:

> "Even as I am sitting here and eating, I cannot avoid concentrating my attention at the very centre of this sphere of Dhamma. Indeed, it is wonderful to observe the stability and security of this sphere of Dhamma. And what brightness too! Even the brightness of the sun is inferior! The light of the sun is as a firefly compared to the huge torchlight brightness of this sphere of Dhamma!"

While he was eating he could not avoid smiling at the overwhelming sense of well-being that derived from this bliss. He was reminded of a saying of the Buddha: "*Natthi santi paraṃ sukhaṃ*" [There is no higher happiness than peace itself]. He thought further about the height of this achievement, realizing that for him this was just the beginning...

The other monks were curious about the beaming face of the young monk Candasaro as he ate his midday meal. They asked him,"Candasaro, why are you smiling while you are having your lunch? To whom are you smiling, brother?"

"No one", he replied. "I'm not smiling at anyone. I'm just thinking of the greatness of Lord Buddha, and I can't avoid smiling with delight."

"Then you brother, could never be accused of being a wastrel", the other monks observed. "Even as you are eating your midday meal, you are still recollecting the virtues of the Buddha. If Lord Buddha were alive today, He would certainly praise you as a worthy one among his blameless disciples!"

Throughout that day he remained in bliss because of the bright clear sphere of Dhamma firmly established inside his body. After his meal he rested briefly, then made the intention to meditate with utmost dedication. That evening he was again prepared to meditate with every fibre of his being. He made this resolution:

> "Whatever happens, if I cannot attain even a small part of the Truth which the Lord Buddha knew, I will sit to the death. If I die, my actions will be a model of goodness for monks and Buddhists of later generations. This will be my virtue, if I should die."

That afternoon after hearing the recital of the *Pāṭimokkha* in the temple along with his brethren, he was extremely happy, knowing that he had repented of all his transgressions of minor monastic rules. His mind was at ease with the rectitude of his conduct.

Later that afternoon it rained heavily, beating down

in torrents. Candasaro Bhikkhu bathed and found that he was detaching himself more and more from the environment. He entered the temple compound later that afternoon. The rain continued to pour uncommonly hard as if foretelling good fortune for this young monk — foretelling the attainment of the goal he had longed-for during all his years of monkhood. The downpour rinsed all the dust and dirt from the buildings and the land, leaving no nook or cranny uncleansed.

In hindsight, this was a portent loaded with meaning. The secret of Dhammakāya meditation that had been lost to the world for thousands of years, was going to be recovered. He sat down to meditate with a strong resolution to dedicate his life for the goal of insight:

> "O Lord! Impart to me the Dhamma which you attained on that day of your Enlightenment. If my Enlightenment will be of virtue and benefit to Buddhism, then please, O Lord! Transport to me the greatest Dhamma: I shall be Thy champion to maintain and uphold the greatness of Thy Teaching. But should my Enlightenment be in vain, of no benefit to Thy Teaching, then Lord, I will sacrifice my life in this meditation, as the only offering I have for Thee."

Then it rained even more heavily. The atmosphere in the temple became damp. He saw a line of ants escaping from a crack in the floor. For a moment he thought that the ants might come and disturb his meditation, so he dipped his finger into a bottle of kerosene and started to draw a circle around himself. But then he realized that he had just dedicated his life for the sake of the Buddha's Teaching. Should he now falter at the sight of a few biting ants? In self-disgust, he set aside the bottle and continued to meditate unprotected.

The bright clear sphere of Dhamma which he had first perceived before his midday meal was still the same size as the yolk of an egg and firmly established at the centre of his body. As he meditated, the clarity of the sphere of Dhamma increased until it was as lucid as a flawless sphere of crystal. The brightness grew more intense until it outshone the midday sun. He contemplated on this object of meditation for hour after hour, from early in the evening until well after midnight. He found that his meditation could not progress any further than the sphere of Dhamma because he didn't really know how to work with this newfound object of meditation. In all his past experience of learning meditation, there had been no master who had described a technique such as this. Then, coming from the silence at the centre of the sphere of Dhamma, there arose the gentle sound of the ancient words, '*majjhimā-paṭipadā*': a technical term from Pali meaning 'Middle Way'. He thought to himself:

> "Ah!...The 'Middle Way'! From my Scriptural study, we define this as 'a way of life which steers between the two extremes of asceticism and sensual indulgence'."

But now this sound came directly from the centre of his body. The centre of the sphere of Dhamma was becoming inordinately bright as if it were source of all the brightness in his body — bright, intense, cool and soothing. The illumination blazed so that the brightness was multiplied enormously, and deep in the brightness of the sphere of Dhamma he knew there existed something else — something he had never known before. Then he started to realise that there must be a hidden meaning to the 'Middle Way'. That tiny spot at the centre of his body might be the doorway to hidden inner dimensions.

He then tried an experiment: by contemplating deeper and deeper at the centre, it started to expand until it reached the size of an egg-yolk. Meanwhile, the former sphere of Dhamma also gained in size until it became so huge that it reached the horizons and then faded away. When he contemplated deeper at the centre of the new sphere of Dhamma, another one appeared at its centre. He continued this experiment of expanding and concentrating deeper at the centre of each successive sphere of Dhamma. More and more spheres appeared, thousands of them, each one replacing the last. As he meditated deeper, each new sphere of Dhamma was brighter and clearer than the last.

Going yet deeper he could see within each sphere of Dhamma bodies of hidden dimensions of himself. Then, at the end of the succession covering all dimensions of himself, he recovered the key to understanding human nature through all its countless dimensions. At the innermost part of every human being's nature, nested deep within the myriad of multi-dimensional bodies, there exists the body of the Buddha called 'the *Dhammakāya*'. It is of the form of the Buddha sitting deep in meditation. The topknot of the *Dhammakāya* is a lotus bud, beautifully clear and pure. Suddenly, this Buddha spoke in a resonant voice,"That is right!" Having spoken, the mouth of the *Dhammakāya* immediately closed again. The delight overwhelmed him. He whispered to himself:

"Ah!...It is so hard like this. This is why no one else

could manage to achieve it. Sensation, memory, thought and cognition: all these things must be united into one single spot. Once the mind is still, it ceases to be. Once it ceases to be, the new one can arise."

He contemplated further on his finding for a long while, then afraid that his discovery would disappear he sat for a further period of thirty minutes. During this short period while he was meditating, a temple came into his vision. He remembered it at once as Wat Bang Pla, Banglain — the temple in which he had studied long ago as a boy of eleven. At that moment he felt himself already inside that temple — which made him feel sure that in this temple there might be someone ripe for the path.[1]

From the following day onwards, Candasaro took the opportunity to go to Wat Bang Pla, accepting teaching engagements and supporting the ceremonies there until the end of the rains retreat. In the meantime he dedicated himself to this newfound technique of meditation. Going deeper and deeper into the interior dimensions of the meditation he had discovered, he became more and more skilful. The more he studied and practised the meditation, the more he discovered the miraculous within and the Dhamma of Lord Buddha. Meditation in the shrine hall of Wat Boatbon became his daily routine for the last months of the rains.

After the end of the rains retreat, upon receiving Kathina, he bade the abbot of Wat Boatbon farewell and moved to Wat Bang Pla permanently to teach the Dhamma. After four months, three monks (Phra Sangvarn, Phra Baen and Phra Oam) and four lay people attained *Dhammakāya*.

---

1. from *ibid*. p.10

In his thirteenth rains retreat, Candasaro took with him all the monks who had already attained *Dhammakāya* to Wat Songpinong where they were to stay during the rains, teaching Dhamma to monks and interested lay-people. By the end of the rains-retreat, one more monk attained the *Dhammakāya*. After receiving Kaṭhina, he travelled to Wat Pratusarn, Supan Buri province, where his Preceptor, the (now) late Phra Acharn 'Dee' had once resided. Candasaro Bhikkhu stayed there to teach the Dhamma for a further four months before returning to Wat Phra Chetupon.

5
New Incumbent at Wat Paknam

> *"The stopping of the mind is the important thing. Stopping is the manifestation of success in meditation — right from the beginning to arahanthood."*
>
> *(Phramonkolthepmuni)*

In 1916, the position of abbot was vacant at Wat Paknam Bhasicharoen, a temple under royal patronage. H.E. Somdej Phra Wanarat of Wat Phra Chetupon (and monastic governor for Bhasicharoen) wanted to find a secure temple of residence for Candasaro Bhikkhu. His Excellency therefore offered Candasaro the position. At first Candasaro declined the offer but, in the end, like it or not, he had to accept. Before Candasaro Bhikkhu was sent to Wat Paknam Bhasicharoen, Somdej Phra Wanarat forbid him to perform miracles or do anything else that might cause offence to the abbots of neighbouring temples — for His Excellency knew that Candasaro was not of a nature to sit idle but would energize the temple into a hive of activity. His Excellency stressed he had chosen Candasaro for peace among the members of the monastic community. With such an explanation Candasaro had no choice but to accept — originally he accepted with the intention of staying at Wat Paknam for only three months.

On the appointed day, Luang Phaw left Wat Phra Chetupon with the title of acting abbot of Wat Paknam Bhasicharoen. The Department of Religious Affairs provided their motor launch for the passage to Wat Paknam together with four monastic attendants. He was offered the full requisites of an abbot. Luang Phaw was granted the princely sum of thirty baht per month for the first four months and his attendants twenty baht per month each. Somdej Phra Wanarat accompanied him to his new temple. Monks, laymen and laywomen came out to greet him at the canal side in great numbers. At that time he had already received the title of Phra Kru Samu Thananukrom from the local monastic governor.

Thus he came to take the title of abbot of Wat Paknam. His first duty as abbot was to clamp down on the misbehaviour of monks either under his supervision, or affecting the state of his temple. Many of the monks were not fit for the faith of the laypeople. Even the monastic governor of his district and other senior monks were involved in corruption.

Luang Phaw assessed the state of the temple and that night invited the whole of Wat Paknam's monastic community to attend his inaugural sermon as new incumbent abbot in the temple:

> "I have been sent by the monastic governor of this region to govern this temple and advise all incumbents on their conduct using the *Dhammavinaya* as my guide — if the temple is to prosper we must depend on our unity and mutual understanding. None of us was born in this temple. We are all newcomers — to come and abide here is like being cast away without knowing who to turn to for refuge because we are all strangers.
>
> I am certain that the virtue which all of us have accrued through practising in the footsteps of the

> Buddha must bring ease and prosperity to all those practising in the proper way. The majority of you have been ordained for many, many years but still have insufficient knowledge to teach — all you have done is clung like a parasite to the religion without doing anything of use to others. Moreover you have sullied Buddhism in the eyes of the faithful — being ordained like this is like being a hermit crab which wanders spineless from one refuge to another for protection — in such a case what's the use of being ordained, or even coming to live in this temple?
>
> In coming to stay at Wat Paknam, it is my intention to exemplify the *Dhammavinaya* in all that I do. It is up to the older monks here to choose whether or not to follow my example. You can join me or you can do whatever you like. It is not my intention to disturb anybody because we all hold that we are responsible for our own actions. If you choose not to join me, then kindly do not impede the efforts of the others. We are independent but we must all help to keep this temple in order. Anybody who comes or goes must take my leave. We will let bygones be bygones because that was before my arrival, before taking up this post — but now that I am here, I have my duty to fulfil..."

Giving that sermon was like releasing the headwater. For the monks in the temple it had been throwing down the gauntlet. That night in privacy, in front of the shrine of the main chapel, Luang Phaw meditated and then made this resolution:

> "May any monk still to come, come quickly to join this temple. May any monk already here stay all of his life."

The changes, although just, were not to the liking of many locals long used to illicit dealings through the temple. These turned against him and spread mud-slinging gossip. Some even tried to harm him physically. The situation deteriorated to such a point that drunks got intoxicated in the temple precincts and misbehaved, even going so far as to think of plunder and murder as the *bhikkhus* were meeting in conclave. One night eight men came along with the intention of disposing of Luang Phaw altogether, even as he was in the meditation hall. One of the *bhikkhus* on watch went out in defence. Hearing the disturbance, Luang Phaw went out to prevent him. "We *bhikkhus* must never fight nor run," he said. "This is the only way to win at all times." The ruffians backed off into the darkness.[1]

On another night Phra Kamol,[2] a disciple who Luang Phaw praised for his astuteness in giving sermons, was to teach on a subject connected with meditation for the general public. That night Luang Phaw sat in the front row of the hall listening to the sermon too — a compliment in itself to the monk's teaching ability.

On this occasion, Phra Kamol climbed up onto the pulpit (*dhammāsana*). He picked up the palm-leaf scriptures that were to be the subject matter of his sermon. He had only just announced the year[3] when a gunshot rang out in the hall. Phra Kamol hastily

1. from *ibid*. p.11-12

2. The monk was later to be entrusted by Luang Phaw with spreading the Dhamma in Petchburi province for the last three or four years of his life.

3. In the traditional style of preaching, there is a standard protocol for the verses that mark both the beginning and the end of Dhamma sermons. A sermon commences with a statement of the year. It ends with the word *"evaṃ"*.

brought the sermon to an end with the word *"evaṃ"* and everyone looked for the casualty.

Luang Phaw himself had been the target of the shooting. That night an assassin had hidden in the shadows at the front of the pavillion. The bullet had ripped into Luang Phaw's robe and the assassin had made off into the darkness. Luang Phaw remained unmoved. He said, "Such people only strengthen my pursuit of the perfection of patience," and returned to his kuti to change robes. Luang Phaw's robe exhibited two large holes, but miraculously, even though monk's robes are worn snug against the body, his person remained completely unscathed. It was as if the bullet knew the gravity of harming a personality of such importance to humanity, tearing only his robes but refusing even to graze Luang Phaw's body — Luang Phaw's time had not yet come.

The police soon arrived on the scene. They took away the tatters of Luang Phaw's robe as evidence and later caught the culprit, a local villain named 'Rod'. Later Luang Phaw was called to testify in court. With the uncommon compassion of this great master, Luang Phaw attended the trial with his usual impartiality and freedom from anger. He even appealed to the magistrate to lighten the sentence of the accused.

The brush with death was only one of many problems. Luang Phaw dealt calmly with the responsibility for reforming the temple with the resolve, "obstacles are to be overcome" and "difficulties are the grist of perfection." "Being a monk," he proclaimed, "I win every battle without even a fight!"

The pressure was on for Wat Paknam to change. Luang Phaw made it look as if he didn't know what was going on — he made no unnecessary fuss about the changes, but Luang Phaw set the foundation for the formal teaching of meditation to the monks. Luang Phaw was very just. He was not biased, but at the same time his decisions were clear cut and sagacious. He would never go back on his word — the number of temple residents in his care was growing and all had to keep within the limits of their personal discipline or Precepts. It was discipline he relied upon for harmony. Anyone who broke the discipline or infringed the well-being of the others would be warned. If they continued to break the discipline, they would be punished. He said:

> "Force has to be applied to improve peoples' virtues. The mind is like water which always tends to seek its own depth. Without effort, the mind's virtue, like water, will fall to the lowest level — that is the performance of evil deeds. If normal people are to be able to develop their minds to the level of the *arahant*, then effort needs to be made. The mind has to be brought under control until it comes to a standstill. Thus, to govern others, there need to be rules. There needs to be something to force people to become better. There need to be penalties for breaking the rules."

If anyone in the temple broke the regulations or deported themselves in an inappropriate manner, Luang Phaw would warn them for the first offence. He would give them a second warning if they continued to cause offence. If they committed an offence for the third time he would punish them. If they were novices, he would have the old monk Phra Pleaung Chupañña cane them. Sometimes he would punish them himself by having them sweep the temple or cut firewood for the kitchen. If, after all of this, the offender didn't improve he would expel them.

Luang Phaw said it had to be this way, otherwise his time would be wasted negotiating with others instead of making better use of his time in the teaching of high-level meditation.

Luang Phaw saw that the most important virtue needed in the monastic community was unity — and he emphasized adherence to daily routine as the basis of harmony in the temple community — whether it might be daily chanting, listening to sermons or sitting in meditation. Luang Phaw taught:

> "The community should conduct all activities in togetherness — that's the meaning of community spirit. Anyone with community spirit will never fall on hard times. He will never fall from prosperity. Whatever tradition he practises, he'll never denigrate others. But it's necessary to be able to criticise one's fellows in the community and accept their criticism of us as well."

Luang Phaw taught that community spirit brings happiness and prevents infighting, disharmony and serious problems in the community. If problems arise, then they can be easily resolved.

Every fortnight, Luang Phaw made sure that the head shaving of the monks, novices and nuns was performed all on the same day. If anyone didn't shave along with everyone else, Luang Phaw would say,"Even their heads aren't in unison, how can one expect their minds to be?"

If any quarrels arose in the community, he would find out which monks were at the heart of the quarrel and would summon them. He would never ask what the quarrel was about. He would simply ask,"Can both of you forgive each other?" If both of them could get over the quarrel and forgive one another, they would be allowed to stay. If, however, either or both of the parties couldn't get over the quarrel and forgive each other, *both* parties would be thrown out of the temple!

Although Luang Phaw was very strict, he showed loving kindness and compassion to all without any distinction. He taught:

> "...to look down on others, even without realizing it, seeing others as weaker than oneself, speaking irreverendly to them, is like the gables of a house being burned by fire which has spread from the lower storeys. Even the smallest house fire will spread to the gables — in the same way, the resentment of juniors can destroy the person who governs them unless he is compassionate and wishes only happiness to those around him, especially those less privileged than himself."

Luang Phaw always taught his disciples to avoid attachment to the food, clothing, shelter and medicine donated for their use and to be content with whatever they owned or were given. He said they should be like a horse or an elephant that is not fussy about its food:

> "If given hay it eats hay. Given fresh grass it eats fresh grass. Given oats it eats that too. It eats whatever you give it, and eats it with respect and earnest. Monks and novices too, must be easy to maintain, taking whatever they are offered for the happiness of those who donated it. Even Buddhist saints make themselves easy to maintain and are a relief for sponsors of the Buddhist religion. Thus those who are still on the path to sainthood should also make themselves easy to maintain, in order that the life of the religion might be extended."

Not only for monks and novices did Luang Phaw emphasize non-attachment. He taught his lay disciples the art of thrift — to avoid extravagance. He taught that wealth is vital to the householder's life. Everyone has to work hard for a living in order to support their families, however anyone who fails to realize the benefit of thrift, will never manage to set himself up in life. Monks and novices should be easy to support — and laypeople too, should have a standard of living befitting their social status. Luang Phaw taught his disciples the way to make cheap tomyam soup. He said:

> "...make *tomyam* soup from fish sauce. If fresh fish is used for the fish sauce, the sauce will be clear in colour and will have no unpleasant smell. The fish sauce will be sweet and the taste can be adjusted to make it sour, salty or spicy. When you take the soup you should drink only the liquid, but leave the fish intact. When the fluid runs out, simply top up the soup with boiling water, adjust the flavour and drink the soup until the liquid runs out again. Keep on topping up with boiling water until the soup has no sweet fish flavour left. Even then the fish is not thrown away, but used as an ingredient for other foods such as fish chilli sauce to fill it out and improve the consistency."

Luang Phaw taught that the wise eat to live, but fools live to eat.

As the catering, so the lodgings. Accommodation in the temple for monks was very limited.

Newly arrived monks in the temple had to take responsibility for building their own *kutis*. As the number of monks joining the temple increased, a sort of shanty town grew up in every available empty space in the temple. All the monks knew that without accommodation Luang Phaw wouldn't allow them to stay, so they took the only available building material, scraps of wood from the broken coffins in the neighbouring undertakers and built macabre *kutis* which looked more like rabbit hutches or bird-houses than accommodation fit for a monk! The huts were built on stilts over stagnant, putrid water. None of the huts had even so much as a bench or a chair. Most *bhikkhus* had nothing more than a Thermos flask of drinking water.

There was training for monks, novices, laymen and laywomen every day in the evening. Luang Phaw trained the monks to deliver sermons, sometimes alone, sometimes in debate with two or three monks. Luang Phaw would organize sermons throughout the *vassa*. Proper monastic conduct in the temple started to become the norm. The radiance of goodness started to shine in the temple, but at the same time some shadows of suffering still lurked.

Truant children still ran wild in the temple compound and greatly disturbed the life of the monks. The monks were left with almost no spare time to attend to their proper duties. The gangs of children would congregate in the temple and shoot sparrows — an outrage in a Buddhist temple. The children wouldn't listen to reason and would refuse even forceable means to remove them from the compound. The monks had to be wary of the conflict escalating because the childrens' parents were those selfsame neighbours who were reluctant to co-operate with Luang Phaw's reforms. They were the ones who preferred the *status quo*. Luang Phaw observed:

> "These uneducated children are littering up the country — and wrecking this temple in their spare time — they will grow up into hooligans."

Soon he looked for financial support for the teaching fees and set up a community school. Three-hundred children signed up because it was free. Many of the conspiring neighbours realized what Luang Phaw was doing for them and started to accept him. The scruffiness of Wat Paknam started to recede.

About the same time, the reforms begun by King Chulalongkorn to establish government-sponsored primary education throughout the kingdom were implemented in Bhasicharoen. Because the policy of the Ministry of Public Instruction was underfinanced and slow to implement, it started with utilization of the monasteries thoughout the kingdom for the introduction of new texts and techniques.

When the abbot of neighbouring Wat Khunjan passed away, Luang Phaw was designated acting abbot. That temple also had a school and Luang Phaw gradually moved the teaching activities there. In Wat Paknam he developed the old primary school ready for use in teaching Pali and Dhamma for the temple's monks and novices.

Originally the monks of Wat Paknam who studied Pali had to travel to other temples such as Wat Anong, Wat Kalyanamitr, Wat Phrayurawong, Wat Mahathat and Wat Phra Chetupon. In those days the only way to travel was by canal boat. Thonburi, for instance, had no roads. Phraputha·yodfa·chulalok

Bridge had not yet been built. Those studying had to face the same sort of hardships that Luang Phaw himself had faced in his early years — success in one's studies was more closely connected with one's perseverance in attending classes than with the quality of the teaching *per se*. Basically, all the temples did, was provide teaching.

Scriptural study and meditational study went hand-in-hand at Wat Paknam. Luang Phaw had studied both scripture and meditation. Luang Phaw's disciples were expected to do the same. Whoever had special aptitude for the study of Pali emphasised academic studies (*gantha-dhura*). Whoever had special aptitude for the study meditation emphasised Dhamma practice (*vipassanā-dhura*). If anyone lacked either the aptitude to study or meditate, there was always the choice of helping with the administration of the temple. Luang Phaw didn't insist that his monks should study but he *did* insist they be active.

The temple was soon established as a seat of learning. It occupied a newly built, three-storied edifice, 60 metres long and 11 metres wide, and cost about 2½ million baht. The Pali Institute was on the lower two floors. The top floor was for meditation teaching to the public. The building was eventually used by about a thousand *bhikkhus* and novices, not only the resident *bhikkhus* and novices of Wat Paknam, but also those from other temples.[1] Monks from the Bhasicharoen area changed their place of examination to Wat Paknam and were able to take their midday meals in temple's refectory.

One day Luang Phaw returned to Wat Songpinong and met his nephew who was ordained as Phra Kru 'Chua' Obhaso, who was the monastic governor of that

---

1. from *ibid*. p.13

sub-district. Luang Phaw said simply,"At this time, I have found the real thing," and persuaded Phra Kru 'Chua' to move to Wat Paknam. Phra Kru 'Chua' was eager to comply and stayed at Wat Paknam until the end of his days. He was given the honour of sharing Luang Phaw's wooden *kuti* in order that they could meditate together and give Luang Phaw the chance to help heal the other monk's congenital lung disorder. Whatever Luang Phaw discovered in his meditation, he would relate to Phra Kru 'Chua'. Indeed Phra Kru 'Chua' had an excellent memory for Luang Phaw's teachings, both those delivered in front of the congregation and those given in the secrecy of the workshop. Phra Kru 'Chua' was also appointed by Luang Phaw as the keeper of discipline (*vinaithorn*) for the monastic community of Wat Paknam.

The number of monks and novices in the temple increased from the original thirteen to a thousand. The more monks came, the happier Luang Phaw grew — in keeping with his wish on his first night in the temple. Some complained to him that there were too many monks. He would laugh and say, "Now you can see that there must be some truth in the Buddha's Teachings."

He never thought of the burden of finding enough support for so many monks. He laughed as his dream turned into a reality.

Luang Phaw created a segregated, fenced area in the temple for nuns. Each dormitory was occupied by many nuns. No nun was allowed to sleep alone. Luang Phaw prohibited contact beween the monks and the nuns without his permission. If allowed to visit the opposite camp, then the monk or nun in question must go with a companion. Later on, although the number of nuns in the temple grew steadily, there were never any scandals caused by the mixing of nuns and monks. Luang Phaw took close responsibility for everything that took place in the temple — both in public and behind closed doors.

Clean drinking water was plentiful in the temple because Luang Phaw had devised, with the help of Phra Rajamoli (Narong Thitano, late abbot of Wat Raja-orasaram) a water supply system from artesian wells.

Luang Phaw was proud of his achievements. Unlike the forest monk far from the prying eye of the public, everything at Wat Paknam was in the heart of the community and open to public inspection. He said:

> "A flower has its aroma for all to smell — there's no need for me to add any perfume to make it smell better. A corpse doesn't need me to add any putrescence to make its odour offensive — there's no way to hide the smell."

In the same way at Wat Paknam, good or bad, the activities were all accountable to the public. Luang Phaw had nothing and nowhere to hide.

The ulterior motive for many contemporaneous monks in organizing temple activities was to attract promotion in rank according to the ladder of the royal monastic hierarchy. Luang Phaw showed no interest in such promotion. His numerous activities and devotion to the work of training monks, novices and laymen to be real exemplars of Buddhism was solely for the benefit of the future of the religion. Some of the promotion-orientated monks misunderstood Luang Phaw's industrious projects. They saw the scores of young men coming to be ordained each year at Wat Paknam and felt a hint of envy. If Wat Paknam had been a royal temple anywhere else with so many activities, Luang Phaw would have been showered with monastic titles and these in turn would have given him the influence and acceptance to go much further in his work. He received the humble title of Phra Kru Samanatham-samathan in 1921. But as it turned out, the title of Preceptor which he really needed for his work, to enable him to conduct his own ordinations was withheld by the authorities for over thirty years. He would have to wait until 1949 for his first royal title.

Luang Phaw had more immediate worries on his mind. The lack of food for the monks was a regular occurrence. Now that he was abbot of Wat Paknam Bhasicharoen, for the princely sum of 360,000 baht he was able to build a kitchen sufficiently large to cater for a one-thousand strong community of monks, novices, laymen and nuns. The nuns were detailed to run the kitchen. In the beginning rice had to be shipped from the family farm in Songpinong. Later, however, help came from local layfolk and this tradition continues down to the present day. It was the first temple refectory to be built in Thailand. Luang Phaw took upon himself the responsibility to provide for all the monks and novices in the temple. He said:

> "Eat alone and there's never enough — eat together and there will be too much to finish — just you wait, success is only around the corner!"

In actual fact, Luang Phaw himself, always had sufficient to eat, because supporters would always single out the abbot for special attention, however he couldn't let the rest of his monks go hungry. That was why he had to set up a refectory for the meditators and scripture students — the first of its kind in Thailand. Luang Phaw started to provide for the monastic community in 1916 and continued to do so for another forty-three years.

In fact many miracles were associated with Luang Phaw's ability to provide for his temple-goers. One day, in the mid-forties, Uncle Poong collected the remainder of the food left on Luang Phaw's tray after he had taken his midday meal. Usually an attendant would consider it auspicious to subsist upon the remnants of the food left for him by his master. Normally there would be barely enough food left on the tray for one of the attendants. On that occasion, Uncle Poong was about to take the tray for washing, when almost all of Luang Phaw's close attendants, Prayoon Sundara, Plaeng, Kela and Orr turned up, also hoping to take their lunch from the abbot's leftovers. That day, strangely, no regret crossed Poong's mind as he ladled plateful after plateful from the abbot's small rice pot. He felt as if the kindly warmth of the abbot never failed his disciples even at times when by all normal circumstances they ought to be fighting over his scraps...

When Luang Phaw was asked how he managed to provide enough food for so many monks every day, for so many years and still manage to build institutes and other buildings around the temple, he replied:

> "We are the sons of Lord Buddha. When body, speech and mind are pure, we have the right to use the legacy of the Buddha — all through this lifetime. If we weren't truly pure, even if we were to take his legacy and use it, the fruits wouldn't last for long..."

6
Teaching the Tradition

"Ever since being ordained in my youth and after all these years in the monkhood, there is nothing more sacred than meditation in the Dhammakāya tradition."

(Phramonkolthepmuni)

Although Luang Phaw's life was heavily burdened with commitments, he kept to a strict daily schedule in order to perform all the duties expected of him without sacrificing time for instructing his close disciples in meditation. He would instruct the monks and novices in their morning and evening chanting and give a sermon on the *Dhammavinaya* to the assembly morning and evening. On Sundays and quarter-moon days he would preach in the main chapel. He would supervise the teaching of advanced meditation. At 2.00 p.m. on Thursdays he would teach meditation for the benefit of monks, novices and laypeople in the main hall, with a cumulative total of at least 40,000 people coming for tuition over the course of the first fifteen years — only during the Second World War did he shift the venue for meditation teaching to the house of Nah Saiyud Peankertsuk, close to the temple — but teaching went on interrupted and returned to the Vihara again after the War. He would organize the teaching of Pali and scripture in the Pali Institute. Last, but not least, he would receive guests after the midday meal at noon and again in the evening at 7.00 p.m..

Practising meditation according to the prescribed methods — the ultimate practice known to Buddhism — until the supramundane level is attained, will bring the practitioner eternal happiness. Even if the meditator doesn't reach the supramundane, it will still bring them the benefits of purity of body, speech and mind — freedom from greed, hatred and delusion, steadfastness in the Buddhist principles and invulnerability to the ways of evil. So pure were the minds of the monks, novices and nuns residing at Wat Paknam as a result of meditation, that they were often accused of powdering their faces. Little did those uninitiated people know, that the bright and radiant complexions of the Luang Phaw's disciples was one of the byproducts of their meditation practice!

Luang Phaw practised in order to eradicate the roots of all evil. He practised according to the Middle Way and was not corrupted by fame. He always worked for the common good, weighing up the best use of his time. Sometimes he would be invited to receive a meal at someone's house or make a journey where he would have to stay away from the temple overnight. He would rarely accept, preferring to spend his time giving training or meditation instruction. Whenever someone asked whether he would accept an invitation outside the temple, he would ask in return whether it would be possible for another monk to go in his place!

Luang Phaw was also widely admired for his strictness about the handling of money — even those funds that had been donated to him for personal use. Every last baht was turned over to his trusted attendant, Uncle Prayoon. Although he had elegant and expansive buildings constructed for the Pali Institute and for meditation, he never built anything extravagant for his personal use. His own *kuti* was a simple wooden construction — and even this he shared with another monk — Phra Kru 'Chua'. Someone once asked him why he never built anything for himself. He replied that he was already happy with what he had — why not bring happiness to others instead?

He had his mission and he had the courage to pursue it. His aim was to make the training he gave continuous. Life was too short by his standards. His life was always filled by good deeds and he would recall these deeds for others to hear regularly. He wasn't afraid of those who accused him of boasting but believed that true virtue should be brought out in the daylight for all to see. The only things not worthy of repetition were the fake good deeds made up by those with nothing to boast.

For Luang Phaw, the happiness of enlightenment through attaining *Dhammakāya* was beyond words. In the words of one of his disciples:

> "The happiness of meditation is like tasting delicacies in the different levels of a tiffin set. You taste the food in the topmost caddy and it seems delicious — but when you taste the next dish down, it is even more delicious than the first. The third is tastier still. Each successive dish becomes progressively more delicious — just as the Buddha taught that we have to renounce evanescent happinesses in order to attain true happiness."

Luang Phaw said that the bliss of meditation is so great that:

> "...if you have strong health and no anxieties in your mind, you can meditate going through the

centre of the centre for seven days and seven nights without turning back. You will discover unspeakable happiness!"

The happiness of meditation was an achievement all people could share. Luang Phaw took the responsibility for teaching all-comers the Way to *Dhammakāya*. The news of his activities spread to Somdej Phra Wanarat. One day the Somdej called him to task, saying, "Don't be crazy, old fellow! Don't you know that nowadays there are no more *arahants* in the world? Better come along and help us to administer the Sangha!"

Luang Phaw knew that his old teacher wished him well — but the Dhamma of *Vijjā Dhammakāya* was profound, and if one did not perceive its profundity it was only natural to be without faith. Thus he listened to the Somdej's criticism with respect — but back in the privacy of his own temple continued practising and teaching high level meditation. This brought him into great disfavour with the Somdej.

When the Somdej grew older and fell ill, however, Luang Phaw looked after him well, sending food and bird's nest soup for His Excellency by water taxi at four every morning. Furthermore, he dispatched some of his disciples to cure him by meditation techniques. It was only then that the Somdej saw the worth of reading Luang Phaw's sermons on *Dhammakāya* meditation, which had been compiled and published by layfolk. In his study of this meditation he was assisted by advice from Luang Phaw himself.[1] As a result, the Somdej began to accept the *Dhammakāya* tradition and offered to help Luang Phaw in his work.

Chao Kuhn Bhimolthamm (Choy Thanadatto) of

---

1. from *ibid*. p.12

Wat Mahathat was also punctilious in visiting the sick Somdej. One evening when Chao Kuhn Bhimolthamm came to call, the Somdej appealed to him to prepare the long-awaited papers for electing Luang Phaw as Preceptor. It was not long after that that the long awaited seal of approval as Preceptor was rightfully bestowed on Luang Phaw. As soon as the new title was received, the number of ordinations held at Wat Paknam increased manyfold.

Each day, particularly on Thursdays, hundreds of the faithful would come to Luang Phaw for spiritual help. There were many examples of Luang Phaw Wat Paknam healing the terminally ill. All those whose condition was hopeless would be brought to Luang Phaw by their relatives. Luang Phaw's most advanced students would ascertain the cause of the illness through meditation. If the patient was approaching the end, his disciples would say so. If the reason for the illness was the ripening of the effects of past evil deeds, they would heal the illness by having the patient perform an act of major merit to escape the clutches of his past evil karma. If the reason for the illness was physical, they would use the power of meditation to adjust the patient's internal functioning along with the administration of herbal medicine. He always maintained that he did not 'heal' the patients of their illness through meditation, but simply removed the illness from their bodies. Although Luang Phaw always helped so many people, he always taught that the most amenable to recovery were those already well-versed in meditation. In such cases the mental vibrations of the healer and the patient would be in synchrony and the results would manifest themselves quickly.

One such example was a Muslim family in which

the elder sister was a strict adherent to her own faith. The woman's neck erupted in septic boils, resistant to medical treatment, whether conventional, homeopathic, herbal or witch doctors! The boils continued to spread unabated causing her extreme distress.

The patient was taken by her mother to several doctors until finally she was advised to visit Luang Phaw Wat Paknam. Luang Phaw had the reputation for being able to cure hopeless cases, irrespective of race or creed. The mother took her daughter to pay respect to Luang Phaw. Luang Phaw observed the patient and then fell silent for a moment. He said:

> "These are the sort of boils they call 'boils of mercy' because there is no need for the sufferer to visit a doctor. All you need to do is repeat '*Sammā-arahaṃ*' and imagine a crystal ball.[1] In only another seven or eight days, you'll reach 'mercy', so just carry on with this meditation exercise."

He instructed them in meditation there and then, before telling them to return home.

The daughter practised in earnest and found that the pain abated. Whenever the pain returned, she would again meditate and it would disappear. Although the pain could be controlled, the feverish symptoms remained rampant and worsened day by day. The doctors were frightened by the hopelessness of her condition but the patient herself showed no sign of discomfort.

---

1. Luang Phaw saw that the mother and daughter were Muslim and advised them to use a crystal ball rather than a Buddha image to avoid alienating them.

On the fifth and sixth days, the daughter said nothing, but continued with the mantra *'Sammā-arahaṃ'*, her eyes brighter and happier than ever. The fever died down but the boils continued to spread. She refused the medicine others brought her, telling them not to waste their money. She informed her mother that in two or three days she would be leaving.

On hearing these words, everyone in the house broke into tears and tried to comfort her with soothing words. The daughter told them to save their words of consolation because she knew her time had come. She even requested that everyone in the household should meditate on the words *'Sammā-arahaṃ'* — but no one was interested.

On the last day of her life, the doctor came to call and after an examination pronounced her case hopeless. The mother and the patient's sister came to her and told her to recite the word 'Allah'. The patient said, "No, no! It should be *'Sammā-arahaṃ'*!"

She requested that after her demise her mother and sister visit Luang Phaw Wat Paknam and tell him that *'Sammā-arahaṃ'* really helped — because now she could see the Buddha inside. She finished speaking and a few moments later passed away peacefully.

After the funeral, the mother and the younger daughter visited Luang Phaw and passed on the message of farewell and relayed that she had seen the Buddha inside — whatever that meant.

Luang Phaw exclaimed, "Didn't I tell you so? . . . boils of mercy!"

He went on to say that this would be the final lifetime in which the daughter would be plagued with this illness — from now on she would make her way towards Nirvana because she had already attained *Dhammakāya*.

The younger sister said she suddenly felt very inspired by Buddhism — because in spite of her sister's being a strict Muslim, that same sister had changed her religion beyond recognition within such a short space of time. The younger sister practised meditation regularly from that day on and within a month was also able to attain *Dhammakāya*. Her mother followed suit and changed her religion to Buddhism, while culturally still remaining within the Islamic community.

Luang Phaw always maintained that those meditators who helped heal others should always make sure that they themselves were pure.

Luang Phaw was called upon to heal layfolk so often, that in later years he made it known that the sick no longer had to come for audience in person. All they had to do was to send him a letter or leave a note in a box for that purpose located in front of his *kuti*, stating their name, time and date of birth, and the nature of the illness. That was enough. Long distance healing by mind continued to yield miraculous results in the case of the terminally ill.

Even when he was aged, he would still give great importance to providing for the guests to his temple saying, "If I don't help them — then who will? They expect me to be their refuge..."

While inundated by guests, Luang Phaw still had the compassion to ask after the health and prosperity of members of his congregation in their absence, taking responsibility for all of his disciples, however lowly, like a shepherd tending his flock.

It was traditional then for laypeople in need of

funds to consult monks of repute before choosing lucky numbers for the national lottery. When coming to Wat Paknam, however, such people would be disappointed because Luang Phaw taught:

> "Wat Paknam has no holy water, no lucky numbers, no spells, no fortune telling. All we have is the stopping of the mind! What do *you* want from the Buddha's Teachings — the bark or the heartwood?"

Shortly after the World War II, around 1955, black market lotteries were rife in Thai society. Normally anyone asking for luck on the lottery would be chased out of the temple. One day however, a regular in the congregation, who practiced meditation sporadically and had more than a modicum of intelligence came to Luang Phaw asking for lucky numbers to ameliorate his poverty. Luang Phaw didn't say a word, but turned to one of his novices for paper and pencil. Luang Phaw scribbled briefly on the paper and sealed it in an envelope. The layman put out his hand to receive the envelope but Luang Phaw withdrew the envelope from reach saying:

> "Don't you forget, this lottery is going to be the most important of your life. It will help you both in this lifetime and the next. It'll bring you riches both this life and in the hereafter."

The laymen was ecstatic, smiling broadly and thinking of his riches. Luang Phaw had his conditions however:

> "Don't forget . . . no rushing to open this envelope! Wait until you get home. Take a wash and freshen up. Have a good meal. Do your evening chanting. Sit for meditation until your mind is as clear as a diamond. Don't dare to open the envelope if your mind isn't clear — otherwise you'll miss out on worldly success. As soon as your mind is clear, only then open the envelope."

As soon as the layman stepped down from the pavillion a crowd gathered round him. Some people fought with one another in order to get the best price to buy the envelope from him. He refused to sell it. There was no way he was going to give up his lifetime's riches.

He went home and without telling anybody bathed and had a meal and kneeled down to do his chanting. His wife and children said nothing but noticed he was meditating with much more earnest than usual. As soon as he thought that his mind was clear, he whipped out the envelope and prepared to receive his lucky number. He cautiously opened the envelope and took out the slip of paper. On the paper were written nine words: *"The more you gamble, the more you rob yourself."*

He nearly had a heart attack — he was so angry! If Luang Phaw wasn't going to help on the lottery, why didn't he say so? Why did he have to insult me, too? Next he felt regret that he hadn't sold the envelope when all those people had offered to buy it. However, the peace of mind from having just completed his meditation still pervaded his being and he started to think, "If Luang Phaw has gone to such lengths just to teach me a lesson, it means I must have no chance for luck on the lottery."

From that day on he lost all interest in the lottery. All his old lottery friends who used to be wealthier than he, gradually went bankrupt, one-by-one. Some never won the lottery. Others won but the lottery refused to pay and died in the ensuing stabbing matches. The layman continued with the task of earning an honest living and from successful business and from the money he saved by not buying lottery tickets he soon became wealthy and contributed to the temple's upkeep. At last he realized that Luang Phaw hadn't tricked him with promises of fortune all those years ago, but had wanted him to realize his *true* wealth, rather than letting the lottery gobble up his income.

Luang Phaw was famed for the accuracy of his prophecies. Unlike many others, he had the courage to make his prophecies public, whether they were matters concerning himself, his disciples, the temple, the nation or even the world. He knew that his prophecies were reliable — and would make them known so that those around him could prepare themselves. Some criticized him for risking his credibility by making prophecies in public, but he maintained:

> "When we have studied the Teachings of the Buddha to such depth, we know that what the Buddha taught is the truth. The *Dhammakāya* could never mislead anyone."

No matter how prophetic vision or knowledge might arise for Luang Phaw as a result of his meditation, he would relate it to others without exaggeration or interpretation.

The monks' standard of living gradually improved as the reputation of Luang Phaw and the temple spread. In one case related by H.H. the Supreme Patriarch of the time Somdej (Pa) Bun Punnasiri, someone came to Luang Phaw asking, "How many *kutis* will be sponsored by the temple patrons today?"

At that time, the Supreme Patriarch was just an ordinary monk in the rank and file, listening as Luang Phaw received guests. Luang Phaw sat quietly for a moment. He didn't so much as close his eyes, but answered, "They'll sponsor four or five *kutis*."

The future Supreme Patriarch felt very anxious for Luang Phaw. If supporters came and sponsored the exact number of *kutis* Luang Phaw had predicted, there would be no harm done — but what if no one came to sponsor *kutis* today, or the number of sponsors turned out to be more or less than Luang Phaw had predicted? — that would be very damaging indeed to Luang Phaw's reputation. However, moments later a lady and her friends came and sponsored the building of five *kutis* — inspiring the faith of the Supreme Patriarch in the precision of *Vijjā Dhammakāya* from that day to this.

Luang Phaw Wat Paknam not only knew what was going on in the minds of others, he also knew how mature or seasoned his disciples were in the perfection of good deeds — whether they had been pursuing the perfection of good deeds continuously over the course of many lifetimes or whether they their interest in virtue was simply a passing whim. He knew when others were due to attain *Dhammakāya* — as the culmination of perfections pursued over the course of many lifetimes. Luang Phaw had a method of testing the potential of others to attain *Dhammakāya*.

One day in the afternoon, as Luang Phaw was receiving guests, a dark-skinned man of Indian descent, called 'Bang', came to visit having heard Luang Phaw's reputation. He bowed down in respect to Luang Phaw and asked if someone 'of the likes of himself' were to try meditation, whether he would have any chance of attaining *Dhammakāya*. Luang Phaw said that he had a good chance because he must already have performed a lot of perfections in his past to have gained the chance to meet up with Luang Phaw. Where most people would have interpreted this as flattery, Bang trusted Luang Phaw's judgement and questioned Luang Phaw further by asking, "So how many more days will it take me to attain the *Dhammakāya*?"

Luang Phaw sat in meditation for a moment and answered, "If you sit in meditation for an hour a day, it won't take many months."

Bang responded disappointedly,"Does it have to take as long as a month? I'm returning to India tomorrow! Can't I attain *Dhammakāya* today?"

Luang Phaw sat in meditation for another instant, then opened his eyes and said,"It's possible — but there are certain conditions. You must sit for meditation with me here. For as long as I don't leave off from the meditation, you mustn't move. Alright?"

"Okay," Bang agreed.

Luang Phaw sent Bang to wash his face, freshen up and go to the bathroom, then taught him how to meditate, re-emphasizing that, "So long as I don't get up, you mustn't move. If you want to attain *Dhammakāya* today, you have to undergo a special process of seasoning — is that agreed?"

Luang Phaw told Bang to sit for meditation. Bang

did as he was told and sat in earnest. He really wanted to attain *Dhammakāya*. After half-an-hour Bang peeked at Luang Phaw and saw him still sitting unmoved. He closed his eyes again and continued with his meditation. After an hour, he took another peek. His own body was bathed in sweat. Bang persevered. Just after the first hour was up, Bang began to shake. His arms and legs trembled because never before had he sat for extended meditation. Bang opened his eyes and looked up at Luang Phaw. Luang Phaw continued to sit unmoved.

Bang was only forty or fifty years old. Luang Phaw was over seventy. Bang made up his mind, seeing the old monk unmoving, serene, with such a bright complexion, devoid of any sign of physical discomfort, to sit for another full hour in spite of the fact that his body was shaking uncontrollably. Suddenly the shaking stopped. Sweat no longer bathed his body. It must have been about half-past-three when Bang overcame his mind. Bang's dark skin gained a certain radiance. All discomfort ceased. Tension disappeared and his body relaxed. Luang Phaw asked, "Can you see the brightness clearly?"

"Sometimes clearly, sometimes not," replied Bang.

"Maintain your mind at a standstill at the seventh base of the mind in the centre of your stomach," Luang Phaw explained.

The rest of the audience who had joined Luang Phaw for meditation had dwindled, leaving only a few old regulars. After a while Bang said that everything was now clearer. Luang Phaw told him to rest his attention at the centre of the clear sphere at the centre of his stomach — that which is called the sphere of *pathama magga*. A little later Bang asked why he could see himself sitting inside his own stomach.

"Go further into the centre," instructed Luang Phaw.

"I can see the Lord Buddha inside my stomach," reported Bang.

"That's it," exclaimed Luang Phaw. "You've attained the *Dhammakāya*."

It had taken Bang from 1.00 p.m. until 4.00 p.m. to attain *Dhammakāya*. He bowed down before Luang Phaw with the utmost reverence. Luang Phaw asked what time his flight left — because Luang Phaw said he wanted to see him off himself. The others who were sitting with Luang Phaw wondered what Luang Phaw was planning, since he had never seen anyone off at the airport before.

Three to four months later, Bang came back to visit Luang Phaw again and came bearing a neatly wrapped gift for Luang Phaw. He paid obeisance to Luang Phaw in the usual way and announced, "I've been to India and brought a present for you — why not guess what it is?"

Luang Phaw laughed and said, "An apple — just what I wanted." A wave of excitement passed through the onlookers.

Bang asked, "How come the day I left Don Muang airport, you were standing at the foot of the stairs at the aeroplane, but when I raised my hands in respect you disappeared from sight?"

"Only my astral body went to send you off! The real Luang Phaw was here in the temple all the time!"

"And when I arrived in India, you were there to meet me!"

Some people wondered why Bang attained *Dhammakāya* after only a single session of meditation. Bang disclosed, "I saw how much older than

I Luang Phaw was and so thought — soldiers know when they go into battle that they must die, but are still prepared to fight to the last: all I had to fight against was physical discomfort — and if in such workaday conditions I wasn't prepared to put up a fight — better that I die!"

When Luang Phaw built the Pali Institute, he made 84,000 Buddhist amulets. He mixed powder with the ointment of many scented flowers and put the mixture on the shrine to be the subject of homage morning and evening. The mixture was then sun-baked and mixed with more powder before being stamped into amulets as souvenirs for those who came to make donations to the temple. The amulets turned out to be extremely popular with the temple-goers because Luang Phaw had consecrated them himself over the course of a full year through his meditation together with selected disciples all of who had already attained *Dhammakāya*.

Originally, the amulets were distributed only to the initiates of the temple. The distribution wasn't publicised. It was only later when word spread, that hundreds of people came to the temple daily to receive the amulets. Luang Phaw distributed the amulets himself. Only those who made donations at the temple and had the merit receipt to show Luang Phaw were allowed to receive an amulet.

As the word spread, even those from distant provinces came in huge groups to visit the temple. Some chartered passenger barges. If people came at the wrong time, they would have to wait until the next day before receiving their amulet. The temple started to receive an average of 1,500 people per day coming to collect amulets. It was believed that the amulet was not sacred unless collected in person from the hands of Luang Phaw.

Whether a person made a donation of a thousand baht or of ten-thousand baht, they would receive only one amulet, no more. When Luang Phaw was asked the reason, he said that the holiness of the amulet was beyond price. A thousand baht or ten-thousand baht were nothing compared to the real value of these amulets.

The first set of 84,000 amulets was exhausted in less than a year and Luang Phaw produced a second set to satisfy the supporters coming to the temple. Even when Luang Phaw was seriously ill, he still ordered more amulets to be produced and, in spite of his faltering health, distributed the amulets in person. Only when his health was at its weakest did he delegate distribution of the amulets to his disciple Phra Kru Samanatham-samathan (Luang Phaw Lek, Thira Dhammadharo) who had attained *Dhammakāya* since being a novice, could heal others through meditation and could teach meditation to Luang Phaw's satisfaction. The amulets continued to enjoy popularity even when Luang Phaw could no longer distribute them himself. Luang Phaw didn't like people to be inspired simply by miracles or sacred objects. He saw his own amulets as something higher — made special, somehow, by the purity of those in the temple. He would never fail to remind those who received these amulets that the Buddha image they were about to wear could do nothing to protect them if they did not themselves practice generosity, keep the precepts and train themselves in meditation using the image as the object of their meditation.

Someone once asked Luang Phaw what he should do if he wanted to attain *Dhammakāya* within three days. Luang Phaw said that all he needed to do was:

"...let the mind come to a standstill and do not be afraid of the sensation of dying. Tell yourself, 'as long as you're not ill, you cannot die'."

Without fail, on Sundays, quarter-moon days and Thursday afternoons at Wat Paknam's three-storied meditation hall (which also served as the Pali Institute) Luang Phaw would teach meditation to the assembled *bhikkhus*, novices, resident laypeople and public at large.

Luang Phaw would commence his teaching by enquiring whether those in the congregation considered themselves upholders of the Buddhist faith or not. If so, then they had the twofold duty of scriptural learning (*gantha-dhura*), and meditation (*vipassanā-dhura*). Of the two, meditation was the most important, because it was the way to liberation from suffering. This was the reason why Luang Phaw always emphasized meditation. It was important to know clearly about the mind because the purpose of Luang Phaw's teaching was to help his disciples purify themselves of defilements.

After preaching thus to the gathering, Luang Phaw would order the candles and incense in front of the shrine to be lit. He would then lead the congregation together in worship, reciting '*Namo-tassa...*' three times in homage to the Buddhas of the past, present and future. The chanting continued with a request for forgiveness of transgressions committed by body, speech and mind against the Triple Gem. He would explain that since they had cleansed their hearts, their consciences were now clear.[1] Finally, there would be the request to all the Buddhas, Dhamma and Sangha, to establish themselves within the mind of each of the congregation. He would then tell everyone to adopt a comfortable posture for meditation.

1. from *ibid*. p.27

Pointing to a figure drawn on a blackboard, he would explain where and how to concentrate the mind. There were two aids involved in concentration: repeating the mantra (*parikamma-bhavanā*) and visualizing the object of meditation (*parikamma-nimitta*). The word used in the first instance was '*Sammā-arahaṃ*'. The object was a sphere. Luang Phaw would take a crystal ball in his hand and display it before the assembled congregation, telling all to visualize the crystal ball beginning by visualizing the sphere at the nostril (left nostril for women, and right for men). This was called the first base of the mind.

As the mind's eye was concentrated at this first base, they were to recite silently '*Sammā-arahaṃ*' three times, fixing attention on the crystal sphere centred at the first base — then mentally shift the sphere down to the second base at the corner of the eye. Slowly, with ease of breathing, mentally recite '*Sammā-arahaṃ*' three times, then shift the sphere to the third base, at the centre of the skull, reciting the mantra three times. The same procedure was followed, shifting the attention down again to bases four, five, and six,[1] with repetitions of the same mantra. The attention was not to veer from the mark. The mind was finally to settle at centre of the body on a level with the navel.

After repeating the mantra three times, one should raise the sphere two finger-breadths above the navel. This was the seventh base of the mind. There were to be found five elemental centres: the earth element to the right, the water element in front, the air element to the left, and the fire element to the back. The space element occupied the centre of the seventh base. In the centre of the space element rested the cognitive element (*viññāṇa-dhātu*),[2] and

---

1. see page 157

2. from *ibid*. p.28

the sphere called the first path (*pathama magga*).[1] The mind was to be concentrated right there at centre, and the mantra *'Sammā-arahaṃ'* recited repeatedly in silence, without allowing the attention to wander. If the attention wandered, it should gently be brought back to the centre.

The aim of meditation was to concentrate in this fashion until inner light appeared. When that light appeared, one had to maintain the stillness of the mind. If any other mental object appeared, be it a leaf, a flower, or a cloud, one had to scrutinize it carefully in a detached way. The object would change by itself without discursive thought. If nothing was seen, the meditator should not be disappointed, because eventually the ability to see clearly with the mind would arise spontaneously. No need for doubt, nor to be excited at any vision — but to be still and gaze at things with equanimity.

After witnessing things change according to conditions, a small sphere, translucent and bright would eventually be seen floating in the centre. This was the sphere of *pathama magga,* the commencement of *magga* (the path), *phala* (the fruit) of the inner way to Nirvana. The mind should be maintained at the centre thereof. After a time, a refined form would appear. And, later, the celestial form, the Brahma form, and the Arūpa-Brahma form. On no account should the attention be allowed to shift outside the body. It should always be kept inside.

Whether seated, reclining, standing, or walking, one should keep the mind concentrated at the centre of the seventh base of the mind. It was permissable to sit in any position so long as one was comfortable

---

1. see definition p.147

— but to sit in the regular position, with right leg crossed upon the left, right hand on the left, palms up, right index finger just touching the left thumb, was of course the best and most perfect posture...

After teaching the meditation technique at length, Luang Phaw would tell the gathering to carry on by themselves, and he would continue to speak in low tones, aiding them, until eventually his voice died away into the silence.[1] The meditation would last for about half an hour.

Then Luang Phaw's voice would rise anew, ending the session — and palms together, he intoned aloud in Pali:

Sabbe buddhā balappattā
Paccekānañca yaṃ balaṃ
Arahantānañca tejena
Rakkhaṃ bandhāmi sabbaso.

Bhavatu sabba maṅgalaṃ
Rakkhantu sabbadevatā
Sabbabuddhānubhāvena
Sadā sotthī bhavantu te.

Bhavatu sabba maṅgalaṃ
Rakkhantu sabbadevatā
Sabbadhammānubhāvena
Sadā sotthī bhavantu te.

Bhavatu sabba maṅgalaṃ
Rakkhantu sabbadevatā
Sabbasaṅghānubhāvena
Sadā sotthī bhavantu te.

---

1. from *ibid*. p.29

- calling on the Grace of the Triple Gem to protect and bless the congregation.

Monks who practice meditation seldom possess the gift of expression. Those who preached well were more often than not scholars of the written word. Luang Phaw himself, well-versed in Pali, was able to manifest all *dhammas* in the light of his broad background. He would announce his subject in Pali and deliver the sermons in relation to meditation practice, interweaving the discourse with Pali terms to support and substantiate his meaning. He put special emphasis on the Mahā Satipaṭṭhāna Sutta.[1]

Luang Phaw would always teach his disciples to ask themselves the questions, "Who am I? Why was I born? How should I conduct my life?" He would give his teachings in two different ways — through theory and through practice. Luang Phaw would give sermons on theory and would teach meditation as his theory-in-practice.

Luang Phaw taught gradually from the elementary to the sophisticated. He would teach about the realms of existence which are near at hand. Then he would move on to teach about the more distant realms and planes of existence such as heaven, hell and Nirvana. This was only to inspire his disciples to seek understanding of the cycle of existence, and to find a way out of that cycle and enter Nirvana. The Teachings of Luang Phaw Wat Paknam are all potentially verifiable by personal practice and will lead to unshakeable confidence in the truth of the Buddha's Teachings and the firm determination to follow in the footsteps of Lord Buddha.

Luang Phaw used the simile of the underground well to encourage his students to persevere in their practice.

---

1. from *ibid*. p.15-16

He taught:

> "Dig your well in search of the spring —
> Keep on digging, never rest —
> Dig shallow, no water's to be found —
> Dig deep until you reach — and the water flows."

Luang Phaw always maintained that:

> "the power of *Dhammakāya* is like the nutrients that nourish a tree to maturity. If we want a tree to bear fruit, we must water it and fertilize it. In the same way, any man who wants fulfilment in life must train himself until attaining *Dhammakāya*. Not only trees need nourishment, but people too!"

Luang Phaw had the ability to know precisely what was going on in the minds of others. When he gave sermons, many people commented that the material of the sermon seemed to be tailormade to the needs of each individual. Even when he was ill and unable to leave his own room, he knew exactly what was going on throughout the temple.

On major religious festivals held at Wat Paknam such as Magha Puja Day and Visakha Puja Day, Luang Phaw would invite the Buddha Himself to attend the ceremony. Many of the congregation would witness with their naked eyes, the *Dhammakāya* as large as the chapel in various positions, up in the sky above — especially when making the candlelit circumambulation of the Shrine Hall at night — an occurrence that could only have come about through the mental prowess of Luang Phaw Wat Paknam.

On generosity he taught that:

"Giving is something everyone should do, but giving must be done without any ulterior motive — for example, if you give a cat food so that it has the strength just to catch mice for us, that isn't generosity, because the motive is centred on the giver. However if you give in order to relieve the cat's hunger and want no material reward — that is generosity. Giving food to other animals is the same — you must give without the thought of receiving anything in return. If you keep a dog just to frighten thieves away — that's not generosity — you must give honestly, sympathetically, intentionally and think, 'if I didn't give something to it on this occasion, it would die, because it is reliant on us'."

Luang Phaw was very compassionate but would not tolerate lies. He said that a person who lies is one devoid of goodness. He praised sincerity in all things, including the pursuit of virtue.

When Luang Phaw received news that his first sponsor 'Nuam', crippled by old-age had no-one to care for her, he took her into the temple, putting her under the care of his nuns. With thought of gratitude for how Nuam had helped him through his most difficult times, Luang Phaw supported her until the end of her days, and when she passed away he held her funeral in style.

On another occasion there was an old man of strong faith, but of slender means, who came to study meditation. Even with only a small amount of progress in his meditation, he was overwhelmed with joy and went home to bid his wife and family farewell. Partings over, he returned to Wat Paknam with a dried fish to offer to Luang Phaw saying,"I'm offering this fish to you. It's all I have."

Luang Phaw laughed and said:

> "That's how it ought to be. You are now a rich man. You have given everything you have. Just as in the time of the Lord Buddha, Punnadasi offered the last of her dough to the Buddha and before long achieved prosperity. Your dried fish is worth more than any dough — your good deed this day, is vast in merit."

Listening to Luang Phaw's praise, the man asked to be ordained and, as he didn't even have enough money to pay for the monk's eight requisites, Luang Phaw arranged for these things.

Luang Phaw always taught that of all the merits, meditation is the highest. He said:

> "To meditate until the mind comes to a standstill, even for an instant of (no longer than) the flap of an elephant's ear or the flick of a snake's tongue, is a huge merit — more than building ten temples or pavillions — because the merit of building temples although improving the quality of your rebirth still leads you back to be reborn in Samsara, the cycle of birth, death and rebirth."

7
The Meditation Workshop

"Dhammakāya is the prime mover. No other thing is more significant in the whole of the cosmos."
(Phramonkolthepmuni)

Compared to your average temple in Thailand, the regular schedule of Wat Paknam, and the crowds of people attending, would have been considered ample. Most temples would already have been congratulating themselves on the number of adherents and the successful maintenance of a full calendar of devotional events. However, Luang Phaw did not set his standards by the norm. He was always looking for better ways to increase the degree of understanding of Dhamma of his followers. In order to do this, he needed to redevelop the oral tradition of meditation teaching which was falling into desuetude in Thailand. The strength of *Dhammakāya* upon which the renewed tradition of meditation teaching had to be built, lay in the need for each meditator to verify for themselves experientially the success of the technique. The most useful help which Luang Phaw could give the majority of his followers was providing the time, space and opportunity for them to perfect their skill and first-hand experience in meditation.

It was in response to this need that he led the innovative building at Wat Paknam of the '*Rong·ngahn·tahm·vijja*' or 'meditation workshop'. Luang Phaw described the merit of contributing to the building of the meditation workshop as unbelievably large. When he announced his plans to build the *Rong·ngahn·tahm·vijja,* a supporter offered to sponsor the whole building. Luang Phaw forbade this however, saying that it must be the a collective effort because sponsoring even a single plank or a single nail for the building of the workshop would bring incalculable merit day and night, as the workshop had been built in order to bring an end to *Samsara*.

The first meditation workshop was built in a special enclosure halfway between the main chapel and the Vihāra, close to the Tipiṭaka tower. It was a small, wooden two-storey building. The upper and lower stories were connected by a duct sufficiently large only to allow Luang Phaw's voice from the upper level to be audible to those below. On the lower floor there were two rows of six bed (bases) with an aisle sufficiently wide to walk between. The floor was bare earth. By day the nuns would sit in meditation on the bases. By night, mosquito nets would be draped over them to allow the nuns to continue with their meditation unbitten. The same arrangements were made on the upper floor, too, but only Luang Phaw, monks and novices were allowed there. There were no stairs between the upper and lower floors and the entrances to the two floors were separate, so that the male and female meditators had no chance of seeing each other, let alone meeting.

The second workshop was a square, single-storey building composed of two twin rooms, side-by-side and separated by a thin partition. Each room was sufficiently large to hold forty meditators. The right hand room contained laymen (*upāsaka*) and monks. The left-hand room contained nuns and laywomen (*upāsikā*). Luang Phaw had a place at the front of the building, on the right-hand side next to the partition. Luang Phaw gave instructions for the meditation group through a slit in the wall allowing the *upāsikā* to hear his words without being able to see the speaker. Again, the entrances to the two sides of the room were separate.

Luang Phaw designated that this hall be used by meditators, for twenty-four hours-a-day, seven-days-a-week. The abbot selected only the most gifted of the meditators. Their 'brief' was to devote their lives to the investigation of the spiritual world that lies beyond the path to *Dhammakāya*. The workshop meditators gave up everything — even their own free-time. They had almost no time to sleep, especially Luang Phaw who had to keep up his public appearances for the general welfare of the temple.

During the War, Luang Phaw divided his gifted meditators into two shifts. They would take alternate turns at sitting for twelve hours of meditation each day, six hours at a time, from midnight to 6.00 a.m., 6.00 a.m. to noon, noon to 6.00 p.m. and 6.00 p.m. to midnight. After the War, Luang Phaw began to deploy three teams in six shifts — each shift of four hours' duration. Each shift had its own leader — chosen by Luang Phaw for their discipline. When changing shifts, the incoming meditators would arrive half-an-hour early to 'warm up' their minds and benefit from the spiritual energy generated by the outgoing shift.

Luang Phaw's advanced Dhamma teachings were suitable only for those disciples who had accumulated sufficient perfections over the course of many lifetimes. Such teachings were not suitable for everybody, because only the adepts of *Vijjā Dhammakāya* could work as a team to plumb the subtle recesses of the human psyche.

Shortly after the inception of the meditation workshop a capable disciple of Kuhn Yay Thongsuk named 'Chandra' was introduced to Luang Phaw. Luang Phaw recognized in her an innate aptitude for meditation and greeted her with the words,"What kept you so long?" Without having to pass the usual examinations of prowess in Dhamma practice, Luang Phaw sent her straight into the meditation workshop. Once she had familiarized herself with the unfamiliar language and protocol inside the workshop, Luang Phaw elected her as head of the night shift.

In the meditation workshop, *Vijjā Dhammakāya* was the main focus. In the initial stages this meant an understanding of the knowledge taught by Lord Buddha, namely, the Threefold Knowledge, Eightfold Supra-normal Knowledge and the Sixfold Super-knowledge. Once adept in these forms of knowledge they would apply that knowledge to free all beings from *Samsara*.

The perpetual meditation schedule was unprecedented in that it allowed the wisdom of *Dhammakāya* to be verified again and again.

On three occasions Luang Phaw employed the spiritual power of those in the meditation team to obtain a huge and ancient crystal ball from the bowels of the earth. The first time in the period 1935-6, he detected, through the insight of *Vijjā Dhammakāya,* the presence of a crystal ball the size of a durian, deep beneath the 'white' building in the temple. Luang Phaw knew that this was the sort of crystal that is the symbol of such rulers as the Universal Monarch (*cakravartin*). He said:

> "If only this crystal ball would stay with us, we wouldn't need to bother with this bad old world any more. We could start out on a whole new world and turn everything around. We would all be able to live in comfort, sustained by the power of this crystal ball, without having to earn a living."

He ordered one half of his team to dig down for the sphere and the other half to meditate to pull the crystal ball up. At night, the crystal ball came close to the mouth of the hole, its green light illuminating the white mosquito net placed there — and each night a cat with a diamond eye would come and play in the aura of the crystal light.

Among the diggers at that time was an *aram*-boy of twelve, who later on in life became the abbot of Wat Lamphaya. Luang Phaw placed a clean white mosquito net over the mouth of the hole they had dug and then sat in meditation in the seclusion of his own *kuti*. Each time the nuns dug closer to the crystal sphere, it would sink deeper, out of their reach. Moving freely through the rock with a groaning sound so loud that the young *aram*-boy fainted with fear. At that time the number of meditators in the team adept in *Vijjā Dhammakāya* was still few. They had insufficient power to control the crystal ball and it escaped through the earth.

In the 1940's Luang Phaw ordered his meditation researchers to dig for the crystal ball again. This time they sent a nun who had already attained the *Dhammakāya* down into the hole alone while the rest of the team meditated above. She managed to capture the crystal ball in a white cloth. Again the crystal ball's green radiance shone from the hole. Luang Phaw picked up the crystal ball and enshrined it in the main chapel. They paid respect to the crystal ball with jasmine flowers. The crystal ball was indeed the size of a durian, incredibly clear but gnarled. The crystal ball remained within the chapel for six days and then on the seventh night, an unseasonal storm whipped up around the temple. A tremendous flash of lightning struck the chapel and the crystal ball was gone leaving only the white cloth. Luang Phaw mused:

> "Our perfections are still weak. We have still not conquered the dark side. Our hardship must continue because we are still riddled with defilements. Our wisdom is still imprecise. For this reason the crystal ball has slipped our grasp."

The third time Luang Phaw detected a crystal ball beneath the temple, again the team dug as close as it could. Every time they came close it would sink deeper into the bowels of the earth with a tremendous groaning as it moved inexorably through the bedrock. As they came closer, the crystal ball disappeared and all that was left was a nest of cobras which attacked the nuns, biting them mercilessly without respite. The crystal ball was gone for good. Luang Phaw used meditation to cure the nuns. He protested:

> "They will not fight us face-to-face and yet they will not give in to us."

On another occasion, Luang Phaw brought a mango seed into the meditation workshop, for an experiment on the power of meditation. Since the workshop floor was bare earth, he planted and watered the seed there. Without any warning the seed sprouted and grew to be a mango tree of full height within half an hour, fully leaved and with flowers too! It bore fruit which was golden in hue, exactly like the description of the magical fruits of the Himavanta forest described in the Buddhist scriptures. Luang Phaw divided the mangoes so that everyone in the workshop had some. The taste was deliquescent!

Even though Luang Phaw devoted the majority of his time to teaching and spreading the *Dhammakāya* tradition, he still took his responsibilities for governing the monastic community very seriously. He would walk around the temple every night, checking on the behaviour and wellbeing of the community. He expected to find intruders in the temple grounds — especially when it drizzled continuously. He said there are only two sorts of people who liked this sort of weather at night — thieves and adulterers. He would go out to check on the behaviour of the monks, novices, nuns and others in his care to see if anyone had gone out on midnight escapades — or, conversely, if anyone had been particularly diligent in their Pali studies. Luang Phaw would check all the rooms where the monks and novices stayed.

If Luang Phaw saw light coming from a room and heard the sound of scripture repeated aloud, he would be enormously pleased. He would call that monk to meet him and would inquire about his wellbeing and give him special support in his studies. Some years when an especially large number of students succeeded in their studies, he would organize a ceremony of congratulation, present the monks with new robes and announce the names of the successful monks in front of the congregation so that the temple supporters could share in the congratulations.

If Luang Phaw saw light coming from a room accompanied by the sound of conversation, he would knock on the door and warn the monk to turn off his light. Everyone knew that Luang Phaw was meticulous about the saving of electricity and water in the temple — both were to be used only in case of need. He would turn off the master switch during daylight hours so that no-one wasted electricity unnecessarily.

One night, Luang Phaw passed a room where two monks stayed. He saw light under the door and heard conversation. Outside the room all was quiet. There was no one else around. Luang Phaw knocked gently on the door with the intention to tell the monks to turn the light out. At the sound of the knocking, the sound of conversation suddenly went quiet. Instead of the door being opened, the scared shout came from inside the room, "Go away! I'll transfer merit for you tomorrow."

Luang Phaw said nothing and went on his way. The next morning after chanting, Luang Phaw gave his usual sermon. Normally, if he had found anything the night before, he would announce it in front of the assembly. Anyone who had broken the Vinaya or any temple regulations, would be in a cold sweat at this time. Luang Phaw had a way of letting guilty members of the congregation know that their behaviour had been unmasked. He would make sure that everyone realized that they could not keep their behaviour secret from him. That morning he exclaimed:

> "Just a moment ago, someone among us was very keen on transferring merit — to the extent that he even transferred merit for his Preceptor who has still not left this world!"

In the case that Luang Phaw had any personal criticism, he would deliver it personally — not in front of the rest of the congregation. For serious matters, offenders would be asked to leave the temple without anyone else's knowing.

Luang Phaw continually found new ways of checking the temple at night so that no one could predict his routine. Some nights Luang Phaw would go for his rounds wearing nothing more than his under-robe (*angsa*) and would stand on watch in the shadows with a lighted stick of incense, the glowing end of which looked like a cigarette. No one would pay this monk any attention, for they knew that Luang Phaw would be fully robed whenever outside his *kuti* and never smoked. Once he caught a novice smearing himself with talcum powder and asked casually whether he had spots. The novice said he didn't. Luang Phaw told the novice never to use cosmetics in the manner of a householder again.

For other shirkers, the distant scent of incense from upwind at night was enough to tell them that their laxity had been discovered by Luang Phaw on his rounds.

Another night Luang Phaw passed the nuns' compound. One of the nuns had invited a friend to stay overnight in her room to study the Precepts. Luang Phaw saw that it was already late, but the light in the nun's room was still on. Luang Phaw looked through the window and saw the nun trying on her friend's blouse in front of the mirror and laughing. Luang Phaw picked up a brick and threw it through the window. It was quickly followed by another two. The nun trying on the blouse came running out of the building but could not see anyone to blame, so she shouted, "You can't get away with throwing things at me when I've done nothing wrong! Just you wait and I'll tell Luang Phaw!"

The next morning the nun went to tell Luang Phaw so that the perpetrator could be found and punished. Luang Phaw asked casually what the nun was doing at the time of the incident and why she hadn't put off the light and gone to bed. The nun beat around the bush. Luang Phaw continued with his questioning and eventually disclosed that he had thrown the bricks himself! He taught her that she should never misbehave like that again because frivolity would cause the mind to wander and her meditation would suffer. He taught all his disciples who had renounced the home life to be careful of slipping back into their old habits or their vows would have been in vain. He taught:

"The world is evil,
But if Dhamma is traded for worldly concern,
Nothing is left but eating, sleeping and outings
— Nothing more than these three..."

In spite of his strictness, Luang Phaw kept his sense of humour. He had ways of embarrassing people about personal shortcomings they needed to correct.

Once Luang Phaw accepted an invitation together with eight monks to perform the chanting for the consecration of a new house. There was one verse which only Luang Phaw and one of the other monks, Phra Kru Vichien Dhammakovit, knew. The other seven monks didn't know it. At the end of the chanting, the owner of the house brought refreshments for all nine of the monks. Luang Phaw indicated that the tray of refreshments should be offered to him. He accepted the tray and put it down next to him. He picked up one of the glasses saying that it should be offered to Phra Kru Vichien and it was passed down the row of monks right in front of their noses — while exclaiming:

> "Vichien, only the two of us put in any effort today — let us drink together!"

On another occasion when Acharn Treeta Niemkham had just retired from being a nun, she had a strong desire to perm her hair. She went to ask Luang Phaw's permission first. She didn't think that Luang Phaw would show much interest, but when she returned from the hairdresser, Luang Phaw summoned her. At first she thought Luang Phaw had some urgent business to discuss with her, but in fact Luang Phaw had not forgotten that she had gone for a perm!

He asked gesturing, "How much did that cost?"

"One-hundred and fifty baht, Sir," she replied.

"Err," he exclaimed. "Quite expensive but pretty, I guess."

Treeta was just about to breathe a sigh of relief, thinking that on this occasion Luang Phaw was not going to be as fierce as he usually was about such frivolities — but Luang Phaw continued in a way that quickly erased the smile from her face.

"But I think the hair on my shins is prettier, naturally curled and no need to spend hard-earned money to keep it in order!"

Among the workshop meditators was a thin and wily nun called Mae Chee Nag. She was one of the most gifted meditators. She had purified her mind to a high degree — so much that she had the power to cause earthquakes and her knowledge of the future was impeccable. Whenever she made a prophecy, it was bound to come true. Thus, on the day when Mae Chee Nag said that she *herself* would be bitten simultaneously by three cobras, before 7.00 p.m., the temple attendant Uncle Plaeng was very concerned and immediately prepared an antidote for cobra bites. Between the *kuti*s at Wat Paknam there was an expanse of long grass on either side of the path to the meditation workshop. Mae Chee Nag ordered that no one should leave their *kuti* before 7.00 p.m.. She herself retired to her *kuti* and performed her evening chanting — in those days, the recitation of '*Itipiso...*' 108 times. She was well practiced and knew intuitively, without counting, when she had reached the last verse. This evening was no different — she finished her chanting and looked up at the clock. The clock said 7.00 p.m.. She put on her shawl and went down the stairs to the path. She had walked only a few steps when she was bitten on the arm by three cobras. Her cry roused the others to her rescue. Everyone was surprised to find that Mae Chee Nag was the only one to disobey her own orders. When they took her back into her *kuti*, they noticed that the clock did not yet read 7.00 p.m.. Apparently, in spite of Mae Chee Nag's wisdom, bad karma had undermined her vigilance, causing her to read the time wrongly so that she fell prey to the very misfortune she was expecting!

Kuhn Yay Chandra was the most adept of all the meditators. Whenever Luang Phaw asked her a question, or requested her to do anything, she could fulfil his request. Nothing Luang Phaw told her to do was beyond her ability. If she were asked to look for the afterlife destinations of the deceased, she could do so. If she was asked to look into the future or into the past, she could do it. She was once asked to check on the language of animals. One day when Luang Phaw was returning from lunch, he spotted two pigeons on the temple roof. He challenged Kuhn Yay to find out the conversation which had taken place between them. He said that the two pigeons had been perched together on the temple roof. One pigeon had turned its head to face away from the other, and then the two pigeons had flown off together in the same direction.

Without knowing any more than this, Kuhn Yay went away to meditate upon the *Dhammakāya*. She was able to understand the pigeons and returned to Luang Phaw with the answer. The pair of pigeons had been husband and wife — the male had been asking the female about the route to their destination so that they would not get lost on the way. The female had turned her head away to recollect the route before they both set off together in the agreed direction. Luang Phaw said nothing in response to Kuhn Yay's answer. He had the habit of never praising people for their good behaviour — he would criticize others when their faults needed correction, but would remain silent if there was nothing to correct.

There was only one occasion when Luang Phaw praised his students publicly and that was when he praised Kuhn Yay Chandra as being 'number one — second to none', the most adept of his meditators.

Anybody who has had the chance to study the nature of miracles will realize that they are just an ordinary by-product of meditation practice and visualization. Luang Phaw never, however, intended that his disciples give much importance to miracles. His aim was always to use *Vijjā Dhammakāya* to reach an end of all defilements, to bring an end to the cycle of rebirth and to bring all beings to the sanctuary of Nirvana.

Huge numbers of people attained unalloyed happiness through meditation. Many were satisfied by their results and subsequently left the temple to teach the Dhammakāya technique in other parts of Thailand. However, there was still a small core of especially proficient meditators, particularly among the nuns at Wat Paknam, who stayed by Luang Phaw's side. Like Luang Phaw, the nuns stayed at Wat Paknam and never rested content with their already high level of attainment, because in the words of Luang Phaw:

> "The depth of insight in the Dhammakāya technique is so vast, that meditating for twelve hours a day for a lifetime of eighty years would still be insufficient to exhaust its extent."

Even at the national level, Luang Phaw was given recognition for his success and unflagging zeal. His efforts didn't go unnoticed by either the monastic community or the Palace. He was awarded successively higher monastic titles as follows:

1916 - Phra Kru Samu Thananukrom
1921 - Phra Kru Samanathamm-samathan
1949 - Phrabhavanakosolthera

1951 - Honorary Pali Grade Fan
1955 - Phramonkolrajamuni
1957 - Phramonkolthepmuni

Luang Phaw Wat Paknam was promoted to a very high level in the monastic hierarchy and was eventually officially awarded the royal title of 'Phramonkolthepmuni'.

Luang Phaw's vocation was not without hindrances. The impact of the Dhammakāya meditation was widespread, causing a stir among those used to other Buddhist practices. References to *Dhammakāya* in the Theravāda Buddhist Canon are scant, and Luang Phaw found himself confronted by many people who believed that Dhammakāya Meditation was alien to Buddhism, and that the highest Truth of the Buddha's Teaching had died with the passing of the historical Buddha.

Only much later would Dhammakāya meditation become one of the most popular techniques in Thailand. During Luang Phaw's lifetime, this meditation system caused many points of controversy to be raised among his fellow Buddhists. Some monks thought that Luang Phaw had meditated too much and as a result was teaching something that was not in keeping with Buddhism. At first sight Luang Phaw's teachings didn't seem to correspond with those recorded in the Pali Canon. Such was the absolute profundity of the truth into which Luang Phaw had gained insight that his Buddhist teachings were very precise. Ironically, he received a continuous stream of complaints from a public long used to vague platitudes on Buddhism. However, Luang Phaw, like any 'pioneer', had to treat these prejudices as 'just another obstacle to be overcome'.

Luang Phaw was quite close to the Supreme Patriarch,

and on one occasion discussed with His Holiness the allegations which so many people had levelled against him:

"We are not stupid people who cannot tell the difference between 'what's right' and 'what's wrong'! Why should we tell lies in order to boost our self-aggrandisement in the eyes of others? They only accuse us because they don't know *Dhammakāya* for themselves. They know neither the place where *Dhammakāya* exists, nor the meaning of the word itself! This ignorance can be the only reason why they are so misguided to complain about us who are forthright and sincere in teaching from our own true experience. When ignorant people who don't know the real Doctrine of the Lord Buddha attack our meditation technique, they cannot upset the truth, but will succeed only in undermining the faith of weak-minded people.The real jewel of the Buddha's Teaching is ever-shining and only the wise can look upon it in true admiration.

The results of the truth are derived entirely from the meditator's own experience, not from doctrinal study. At Wat Paknam, the monks in my care, even when eating and sleeping, do nothing in their lives but practise meditation. We talk together about what we have achieved and we are tireless in encouraging others to do good. We do not advertise ourselves in newspapers, but our fame relies solely on our good reputation — but even in spite of the virtue of our temple, people still come to slander us — behaviour that will ultimately only cause more trouble for themselves. We don't ask people to pay for the meditation teaching they receive at the temple. If we reach the truth and guide people in the right way, then in the end skill in meditation will triumph over slander. I am not upset by all this controversy because *Dhammakāya* is the truth of Buddhism. It is real. It will appear to all those who attain to that level of conciousness. My conviction in the veracity of Buddhism is unshakeable."

He quoted the Buddha's Teaching to his disciple Vakkali: *"Yo kho Vakkali Dhammaṃ passati so maṃ passati"* [Vakkali, whoever sees Dhamma, sees me].[1]

He went on to give another of the Buddha's discourses to the novice Vāseṭṭha: *"Tathāgatassa h'etaṃ Vāseṭṭhādhi-vacanaṃ Dhammakāyo iti pi ..."* [O Vāseṭṭhas! The Word of Dhammakāya is indeed the name of the Tathāgata].[2]

The story of Vakkali concerns the novice's attachment to the beauty of the physical body of the Buddha. The meaning of the quotation from the Aggañña Sutta relates to the Nature of that which people experience in meditation and gives the real meaning of the word 'Tathāgata'. 'Dhamma' the absolute truth, is seen to mean 'the Dhamma inside', the *Dhammakāya* or the 'Body of Dhamma':

"The one who sees Dhamma sees the Tathāgata. This means that the *Dhammakāya* or the Body of Dhamma is the real Tathāgata. The one who sees the Dhamma, the *Dhammakāya,* in fact sees the Buddha. The Real Buddha is the *Dhammakāya,* not the physical body of the historical Buddha. Why should Lord Buddha speak thus to Vakkali? Even if a person looks upon the physical body of

---

1. S.iii.120 2. D.iii.84

the Buddha with his own eyes, does not he really 'see' the Buddha? It didn't make any reference in the text to any blindness or physical disability which Vakkali might have possessed. Why then, should the Buddha speak thus? Indeed, the reason for this Teaching is to prevent confusion. Seeing the Buddha with the physical eye is to see the physical body of the Buddha — the body of Siddhattha Gotama who renounced the world to become a monk. This physical body is prone to death and decay. It should not be confused with the real body of the Buddha, which is formed of the very substance of Enlightenment. This internal body of the Buddha is eternal. It can only be seen with the 'eye of *Dhammakāya*. This is a spiritual eye, not the eye of the physical body. The ability to use this eye is a power we develop by cultivating meditation at its highest.

Interpreting the texts directly as I have done, it is obvious that the simple wording which Lord Buddha used contains very deep and subtle meaning. No one except for those who have attained to *Dhammakāya* themselves would be able to understand the depth of this meaning. Thus, I teach all the way to *Dhammakāya*, so that all may find out for themselves the absolute truth that lies within..."

His efforts to spread the Dhammakāya Tradition attracted hundreds of thousands of people as his disciples. Of this number tens-of-thousands were able to attain *Dhammakāya* and helped teach Dhammakāya meditation in the provinces. Those monks, novices and nuns who attained an even higher level of insight in the Dhammakāya Tradition stayed at Wat Paknam to help

Luang Phaw conduct advanced meditation research. He taught the monks and novices:

> "All of you must try to attain *Dhammakāya* first — then I can start to teach you insight. Even if it takes you twenty years to attain it, that's not too late for you to learn something from me!"

8
A Temple in Wartime

When you need happiness, you should bring your mind to a standstill. Stopping is the manifestation of success — it is the real happiness, to which the happiness of no other thing can compare.
(Phramonkolthepmuni)

At the outbreak of World War II, Luang Phaw showed a lively interest in the news. The war changed the lives of everybody who lived in Bangkok and the temple was no exception. There was considerable danger for everybody who lived in the capital. This was the only time in the history of Wat Paknam when Luang Phaw did not teach meditation for the general public inside the main Vihāra of the temple itself. During the Second World War, because of the possible danger for public attending teachings, especially on Thursdays, Luang Phaw moved the venue for public meetings to the house of Nah Saiyud Peankerdsuk which was not far from the temple precincts.

During World War II, Luang Phaw felt that it was not safe for the monks of Wat Paknam to go on almsround. The monks, however, always had enough to eat because the kitchen provided for them. Also Luang Phaw would instruct Kuhn Yay Chandra to have the meditators in the temple invoke the Grace of the Perfections of the *Dhammakāya* to provide sufficient food for the temple community each day. He was certain that each day, there must always be someone of faith to support the temple and he instructed the meditators to facilitate the opportunity for the faithful to realize their wish to donate rice at the temple. Luang Phaw also commented that:

> "In any place where there are those who train their minds to come to a standstill, there will never be a shortage of food. Even if you are a monk practising until you have brought your mind to a standstill in the depths of the forest, you will not be able to escape the generosity of those who seek you out in order to offer sustenance."

Once, the rice in the temple storeroom was nearly depleted — and there was no prospect of a fresh supply for the next day.[1] An additional complication during wartime was that martial law prohibited the transport of strategic materials (such as rice). Even if you were to buy a cargo of rice, it was no guarantee that you could use it as you wished. The nun in charge of the storeroom was at her wit's end, and went to inform Luang Phaw.

She said, "We have no more rice."

"Of course we have!" Luang Phaw told her, "Do not fear. The rice is on its way."

The nun was confused by Luang Phaw's confidence, but at the same time felt uplifted by the assurance that there *would* be rice.

It turned out that the law had been no deterrent to the generosity of temple supporters determined to give alms for the monks in the temple. They used a motor launch to tow a barge from far in the provinces and plied from one side of the canal to the other, collecting donations of food from well-wishers until the barge was full. The cargo of almsfood was then hidden beneath a

1. from *ibid*. p.7

layer of banana leaves and sugar cane before towing the boat downstream to Wat Paknam, right under the oblivious noses of the authorities, to moor in front of the temple. Rice was unloaded by the sackful and carried to the storeroom, filling it up to the amazement of all who bore witness!

Luang Phaw had long been renowned for the special compassion he displayed towards foreigners. If any foreigner were to attain *Dhammakāya* in meditation, he could not cease to express his happiness for days upon end. Luang Phaw extended this same compassion to the warring nations of the War. In spite of the hostilities and the obvious temptation for nationalist feeling, Luang Phaw and his meditators, regarded a world at war with impartiality. Neither nationality nor the occupation of Thailand caused them to view one side or the other as their enemies. They saw all humans as equal and prayed for harmony and an end to the hostilities without bloodshed. Indeed, his standard blessing given to all who attended the temple was that all prosper, that the rice ripen in the fields, that the rain fall according to season and that men everywhere give up fighting amongst themselves.

During World War II, Bangkok was occupied by soldiers of the Axis — more than a million in all. The Allies bombed Bangkok ceaselessly. In spite of the bombing, Luang Phaw did not evacuate the temple. On the contrary, he intensified his activities owing to the increased number of temple-goers.

Wat Paknam was located only a 'stone's throw' away from the lock between the mouth of the Bhasicharoen Canal and the Canal of Greater Bangkok. This was a place of strategic significance and a target for Allied bombing. Luang Phaw had unshakeable faith that the omnipotence of the *Dhammakāya* would protect Wat Paknam and its congregation from the bombs. Luang Phaw's confidence was not unfounded and in reality, neither Wat Paknam nor the adjacent locks were ever to sustain bomb damage. Temple attendance increased because Wat Paknam gained a reputation for safety in time of air raids. The public believed that Luang Phaw had some sort of magic power and before long, whenever air-raid sirens were sounded, the people of Bhasicharoen would hasten to the temple precincts rather than shelter in air-raid bunkers.

Luang Phaw heard the distant explosions of bombs falling on Bangkok and remained unmoved.

"Go and intercept those bombs in case they harm somebody. Have them fall in the ocean instead or in uninhabited areas," he ordered Kuhn Yay.

Indeed, in 1941, many of the Bangkok newspapers gave front-page coverage to the manifestation of miracles at Wat Paknam. One particular incident which riveted the press was an air-raid on Bangkok — the target of which was the destruction of the Phraputha·yodfa·chulalok Bridge. Wat Paknam was within striking distance of this target. At that time the inhabitants of the neighbourhood gazed up at the skies and were surprised to see large numbers of nuns from Wat Paknam floating in the air, intercepting the bombs dropped by the bombers and patting them with their bare hands to fall harmlessly in the water or uninhabited areas of forest. So many people saw the heroic efforts of the nuns with their naked eyes that the renown of the miracles of Luang Phaw Wat Paknam spread far and wide. Everybody saw the efforts by Luang Phaw to reduce bloodshed and encourage harmony amongst his fellow men.

Apart from bombs aimed correctly missing their target because of interception, another reason why bombs fell harmlessly in unpopulated areas was because bomb aimers could not find targets located in the city. Interviewed later in a documentary, one bomb-aimer reported his surprise at continuously being confused — when close to the target, Bangkok from the air would miraculously appear to him looking like a forest or farmland and the mirage would persist until the bombers gave up their mission and turned homeward.

In 1945, Luang Phaw meditated using the Wisdom of the *Dhammakāya* and envisioned a horrendously devastating new weapon. It had been built by the Allies to bring the war in Asia to an end. They were planning to test this new weapon, a bomb, by dropping it on Bangkok! Bangkok was the most obvious target, because so many soldiers from the Axis occupied the city.

"What would happen to us if we were victim to this weapon?" Luang Phaw asked the meditators.

Kuhn Yay Chandra verified that the whole city would be obliterated — razed to the ground. She said that the land would be flattened like the skin of a drum — the whole population anihilated.

On hearing this Luang Phaw ordered Uncle Prayoon to take all of the temple assets and leave — going as far away as he could in seven days. Luang Phaw said, if his efforts met with success, after seven days Prayoon would know and would be able to return to the temple in safety. Luang Phaw spoke of the matter with no one else. He locked the doors of the meditation workshop from the inside — allowing no one to enter or leave. Food and drink would be sent in via the letter box. The workshop group sat for meditation in earnest, in order to try and save the country. For a reason known only to Luang Phaw and his meditators, the bomber and the bomb never arrived in Bangkok. The Allies had for some reason changed their minds. It had taken them seven days of perpetual meditation behind locked doors to influence that decision for the sake of their fellow men...

9

Ordinations & the International Scene

"Dhamma is forthright. It can be seen and known only by the forthright"
(Phramonkolthepmuni)

Luang Phaw never refused anyone who came to him with a request for ordination. He considered that ordination was not just becoming a member of the Buddhist order, but was an ordination of the mind itself.

During the ordination of one Khantiko Bhikkhu[1] Luang Phaw announced in clear and resonant tones:

> "You have now had the faith to present to me the dyed yellow robes that are the victory flag of the *arahants*, as prescribed by the Blessed One, in the middle of this assembly of monks, requesting to become a *bhikkhu* in the Buddha Sasana, as a sign of your good intention to ordain on this occasion."

Luang Phaw paused and lifted up his eyes to gaze momentarily into the eyes of the ordinand:[2]

> Your first duty in this ordination is to arouse faith — that is a firm belief in the Grace of the Triple Gem — the Buddha, Dhamma and Sangha — because your ordination has been granted in the tradition of the Blessed One who established Buddhism. Your first step in the study of the virtues of the Blessed One...

---

1. The account of this ordination was also referred to in Bechert, H. (1966) *Buddhismus, Staat und Gesellschaft in den Länden des Theravāda*, *Part 3*, (Hamburg: Metzner) p.542
2. from Magness *ibid*. p.19

He paused and gazed at the ordinand with his penetrating eyes as though ascertaining whether he was concentrating on what he taught. Satisfied, he continued to preach on the qualities of the wisdom, purity and compassion of the Buddha, impressing the ordinand with depth of his analysis.

He studied the ordinand over and over again, as if trying to impress his image into his memory — however, whenever the ordinand's eyes met Luang Phaw's the eyes of the ordinand invariably darted away from Luang Phaw's intense gaze.

Luang Phaw continued to remind the ordinand of the great merit of this encounter and the merit of becoming heir to the Buddha's Noble Order through ordination. The ordinand shifted his weight to relieve his numbness — he had been kneeling with his hands in a gesture of prayer unmoving for a long time. The ordinand bore up to the discomfort, afraid that he would detract from the merit gained from the ordination. Luang Phaw seemed to understand the ordinand's distress and gazed at him with compassion, as he continued:

> "A *bhikkhu* must first understand what meditation is, because meditation is the means by which the mind can be tamed, guarding against wandering. It is the way whereby stillness of the mind arises and is the basis for wisdom."

He went on to explain about the four elements — earth, water, wind and fire, which constitute the thirty-two characteristics of the human body which the ordinand must analyze and see as unwholesome. He reduced the formula to only five, giving the Pali words, *kesa* (hair), *loma* (bodily hair), *nakha* (skin), *danta* (teeth), *taco* (finger/toenails) — telling the ordinand to repeat them after him, first in order and then in reverse.

All were silent. The ordinand waited for Luang Phaw to place the yellow under-robe around his neck, and order him to retire to robe himself,[1] as is the custom. In other temples there would be no delay at this stage. The teaching of meditation was just a token gesture, and the ordinand would quickly be on his way to the robing room. For Luang Phaw, however, this was the time when the ordinand must make his mind ready to receive the new status of monkhood by raising the quality of the mind into first-hand contact with the Dhamma of Lord Buddha. For different ordinands Luang Phaw would have different ways of leading the meditation, and would lead the ordinand to make as much progress in his meditation as he deemed fit. Sometimes, this would make the ceremony very lengthy. Luang Phaw continued, asking, "Did you take a close look at the hair they shaved from your head before your ordination?"

The ordinand answered that he could remember the tuft of his own hair that he took up in his hand while they were shaving his head, but at the same time wondered why Luang Phaw should be asking such a thing during the ordination. It wasn't in the script. Completely in the dark, the ordinand hurriedly checked his mind to see if there was any special meaning in what Luang Phaw was asking. But before he could discover a satisfactory solution, Luang Phaw continued:

---

1. from *ibid*. p.20

> "That's good. Now close your eyes and visualize the image of that tuft of hair at the centre of your body, two finger-breadths above your navel. Sink it down right in the centre there, in the cross-section between an imaginary cord strung between the right side and the left one and another strung between the front and back — right at the point of intersection there. Follow my instructions carefully."

The ordinand closed his eyes and did as he was told, but his doubts only continued to increase. Luang Phaw continued;

> "Bring all your thoughts, imagination and memory down into the centre there, and observe carefully."

But all was dark as far as the ordinand was concerned. After all, what did Luang Phaw expect him to see with his eyes closed? Waiting to see what Luang Phaw's purpose was, the ordinand meditated still kneeling stiffly before Luang Phaw. Nevertheless, he persisted. Luang Phaw asked whether he could see anything yet in his meditation. The ordinand hastily replied that he could see nothing.[1]

Luang Phaw told him:

> "Bring your thoughts to a standstill. Visualize that tuft of hair. Let the image arise at the centre of the intersection. See the visualization and maintain it in mind. Do as I tell you and you will attain vision."

The ordinand had no idea how long he sat before Luang Phaw in meditation — or how long he struggled to rid

1. from *ibid*. p.20

himself of distracting thoughts as Luang Phaw had instructed. As he struggled for control, he consoled himself with the thought that Luang Phaw must have a reason for taking so much trouble and effort — he would not be wasting the ordinand's time.

To the ordinand's surprise, after a time he did begin to discern something. Slowly it arose in the inner darkness. A blur appeared and gradually became clearer. It became so clear in the end that it was as though he were gazing at it with his eyes wide open — yet his eyes were shut. What was it that he saw? The hair which had been shaved from his head. At this the ordinand became rather excited, unable to suppress his curiosity.

"I can see something!" said the ordinand in a trembling voice.

"You can see the tuft of hair, can't you?"

He thought he had achieved what Luang Phaw wanted — but Luang Phaw had not yet finished:[1]

> "Keep observing it continuously. Observe the detail. Observe what direction the ends of the hair are pointing. Which direction are the shaven ends pointing? How is the middle portion curved?"

The ordinand focused his mind's eye so as to be able to answer Luang Phaw's questions. And as soon as he could observe clearly, he replied. Again the ordinand thought he had come to the end of the exercise. But again he was wrong. Luang Phaw commanded the ordinand to examine his vision further. The ordinand obeyed his command, though not wholeheartedly. After all, hair was hair, and the ordinand had already seen it clearly. What else was there to observe?

---

1. from *ibid*. p.21

The ordinand sat further trying to do as he was told. He consoled himself with the thought that Luang Phaw must have something else in store for him to see...

After a long time, the ordinand gradually began to experience a strange sensation of bliss — as if his body were growing lighter and lighter. Despite his physical buoyancy, his mind seemed quiet, still and perfectly at ease — so at ease that it was difficult to find words to express the feeling. The hair which he had seen in the beginning gradually receded from his vision, and in its place there appeared a circle of light radiating a feeling of wellbeing. Gradually, the circle of light condensed itself. Then it began to expand. This continued for some time, with the circle as large as a coin. Radiance spread out from this circle, and his attention was drawn towards the centre. The appearance was like a clear, crystal sphere, as large as the moon when it rises in an empty sky. Apprehensive that this vision would disappear, he fixed his gaze thereon. He had lost all sense of weariness in his legs, and could not say exactly when and how his discomfort had disappeared.

"Do you see anything else?" asked Luang Phaw softly.

"I see light — a sphere the size of a lime," he responded.

Luang Phaw continued:

> "All right. That is enough for today. Remember this sphere. Whenever you close your eyes, you will see it; whenever your eyes are open, you will see it. You will see it throughout the day. You will always see it. You must be careful never to let it be lost."

When the ordinand opened his eyes, Luang Phaw showed that he was satisfied.

Luang Phaw explained:

> "That clear sphere is the beginning (*paṭhama magga*). It is the path of the Blessed One whereby He attained Nirvana. It is the only path, the straight path; there is no other path. Remember this; never let it perish from your sight."

With these words, he gradually extracted the yellow under-robe from the folded bundle of robes and placed it round the ordinand's neck.[1]

> "Go now and robe yourself, and return to receive the Triple Refuge..."

The ordinand looked up at the clock and saw that he had been sitting amidst the monastic assembly for an hour and a half. For him alone Luang Phaw had gone out of his way to show him how to meditate, to show him the path whereby defilements are shed, to enter the coolness, shade and wisdom that is the Buddha *Sāsana*. For him alone Luang Phaw had kept the rest of the congregation waiting.

Meditators at Wat Paknam practised strictly according to Luang Phaw's guidelines. His disciples were inspired to the degree that allowed *Dhammakāya* to spread to nearly every province in Thailand. Chosen disciples such as Kuhn Yay Thongsuk Samdaengpan and Kuhn Yay Thean Theerawat were given a small amount of money by Luang Phaw and sent to preach in more than eighteen provinces, some as far away as Chiangmai.

In 1954, Luang Phaw called an emergency meet-

---

1. from *ibid*. p.22

ing of all his disciples. He announced that he had only five more years left to live. He appealed to all to continue to persevere with the activities he had set in motion. He said that before long the temple would be enlarged, even though he would no longer be present. His disciples pleaded for him to stay on longer, but he said that he must surely die. Everyone present immediately knew how concerned Luang Phaw was for the welfare of the tradition to have publicly appealed to his disciples to take responsibility for the work — especially for perpetuating and spreading the Dhammakāya tradition.

In the meantime in about 1954, the first television broadcast was made in Thailand. The event was one of national importance, so one of the disciples of Wat Paknam put a television on his shoulder and brought the new invention to the temple for Luang Phaw to see — so that the monks at the temple could keep up with the times. The evening's programming had both news and entertainment. Luang Phaw Wat Paknam had the ability to see the danger even in the slightest phenomena. As soon as Luang Phaw saw the show he slapped his knee and shouted, "Evil genius!"

At that time the congregation was just thinking what a favour they had done the monks and the monks were excited over the new device. They turned to ask Luang Phaw what was wrong with the television — when even the government supported it.

Luang Phaw restated himself:

> "Evil Genius — the damage of the television outweighs the benefits — we Thais especially are lax in our Precepts — this will only make our grasp of the Precepts feebler. Can't you see? We're spreading the work of Māra with this

technology. You might as well call it 'Māra'. It brings vices right into our bedrooms, even when monk's sermons have no chance of penetrating that far — limited by time, place and opportunity. Māra has overtaken us (monks) and gotten ahead — we've been defeated — we've been beaten to the bedroom. In times gone by theatre, opera and musicals were confined to the theatre or at least the fairgrounds. Monks had some say and could at least keep up with the broadcast of sense-pleasures. But now! Now, monks are confined to the temples while sense-pleasure has gotten into the bedroom, inside the mosquito net and onto the bed. We have been defeated by Māra again!"

Luang Phaw continued by explaining that:

"All these things are interfering with the support of the Buddhist religion. Even in the wealthy households the residents have no time to offer alms to the monks because they watch television until late and in the morning they can't get up in time to offer food. Anyone who is wealthy these days has a television. The poor have no chance of owning a television because they're so expensive. In fact that's no surprise because the rich households have always been the least supportive of the monastic community. If people are poor then they don't have much chance to give alms either. Middle class people are the strongest supporters of Buddhism. The rich give alms only on the full-moon days or else have their servants give alms on their behalf — it ends up being the person with the least understanding of Buddhism in the household who gets the merit. As television gets

> cheaper they will be accessible to the middle-class and almsgivers will become few and far between. The amount of alms given in Bangkok is already insufficient for all the monks to survive. If the present condition continues with our own homes full of vice and degradation, not only Buddhism will suffer, but our children's education too, as well as the behaviour of those in society."

Buddhism moved with the times and the reputation of *Dhammakāya* was even spread abroad by travellers coming to Luang Phaw for blessing before making international trips.

Without telling anyone Luang Phaw had long nurtured the wish to spread the teachings of *Dhammakāya* in the international community. At a time when transport to the temple had not even advanced to the level of a roadway, Luang Phaw was making far-sighted plans to acquire an aeroplane for the temple, to send monks off to countries abroad to spread the Dhamma and on the return trip to carry those foreign initiates who wanted to come to Thailand to be ordained.

One of the first *bhikkhu*s from Wat Paknam to travel abroad was Thitavedo Bhikkhu who paid a short visit to England in 1953. Through connections at the Buddhist Society of London he was introduced to a learned journalist and lay Buddhist teacher by the name of William Purfurst (aka Richard Randall) who planned to take ordination as a monk. Thitavedo made the arrangements for Purfurst to undertake training for ordination at Wat Paknam and acted as his guide and translator when Purfurst flew out to Thailand in February 1954.

Purfurst was greeted with excitement by the Thai community because never before had a European expressed the wish to be ordained in Thailand's Buddhist Sangha. He was accommodated in specially refurbished lodgings within the temple compound of Wat Paknam. Luang Phaw gave Purfurst personal tuition and after some initial experience in meditation in the confinement of his lodgings, when he was able to perceive inner brightness at the centre of the body, Luang Phaw allowed him to ordain as a novice. During his ordination as a novice, Luang Phaw applied his usual criterion that inner experience of enlightenment is a necessary prerequisite of becoming a monk. All the monks in the ordination quorum were adepts in meditation and helped Luang Phaw extend Purfurst's meditation experience to attainment of the *Dhammakāya*.

The ordination ceremony took four hours. Again, in the seclusion of his accommodation Sāmaṇera William, progressed with his meditation for five months more, until Visakha Puja Day of 1954, when Luang Phaw gave him the great honour of taking the full ordination as a *bhikkhu* and gave him the name 'Kapilavaḍḍho'. Luang Phaw told his supporters with pride:

> "Tomorrow a westerner will take ordination. He has sacrificed his personal happiness, left his people and crossed the seas to seek that which is good and true. To speak the truth, we Thai are Buddhists, who pay homage to the Buddha *Sāsana*. Is it not fitting that we should seek some opportunity to live with that which is good and true, and not let the days pass by in vain?"[1]

Ten thousand people attended the ordination. Many others were inspired to be ordained.

1. from *ibid*. p.17

Kapilavaḍḍho practised meditation in seclusion for four further months. After this time Luang Phaw allowed Kapilavaddho to start accepting invitations to preach and on 8 November 1954, he was sent back to England in order to search for fellow countrymen interested in ordination. Kapilavaḍḍho preached in London and Manchester and was the subject of many newspaper articles. He set the foundations for the English Sangha Trust (which was to continue to support the work of the English monastic community from that time onwards). Three young men, Robert Albison, Peter Morgan and George Blake, came to him with the intention to ordain, and Kapilavaḍḍho ordained them as novices. In December 1955, when he had managed to raise sufficient funds for air tickets, he brought the novices to Thailand and put them under the same strict regime he had himself undergone.

The new trainees were shown the generous hospitality usual to Thais, and were spoiled so much that they forgot their junior status as newcomers to the community. While the newly ordained monks were seated *à table* enjoying a full-blown English breakfast, their seniors had to sit on mats on the ground with only rice soup as their food. Kapilavaḍḍho took the examination for the position of *anusāvanācariya* and passed. He officiated at the full-ordination of his disciples respectively as Suddhavaḍḍhako Bhikkhu, Paññāvaḍḍho Bhikkhu and Vijjāvaḍḍho Bhikkhu.

It may have been that the foreign monks lacked the sense of respect towards their teacher possessed by their Thai brethren. In any case a misunderstanding arose between Luang Phaw and the foreign monks. In a meeting of the whole monastic community, the foreign monks asked Luang Phaw for special privileges via an interpreter. There is no harm in a misunderstanding.

However, in this case the foreign monks got up in the midst of the assembly and deliberately walked out. In Buddhist tradition such a meeting called by the abbot of a temple must be attended by every monk, novice, nun and layperson in the temple without exception. Walking out of the meeting was seen as the height of bad manners. They were misunderstood as having trampled their respect for Luang Phaw, their teacher, and they could not be forgiven. Luang Phaw was in a terrible dilemma. He knew he was helpless if a similar situation arose again. Luang Phaw said:

> "I cannot let this incident pass by, or else they will continue to trample on respect for everything else in the Buddhist religion . . . they have to know how to conduct themselves in (this) land of monasticism. In the company of others they must learn not to think only of themselves."

Unfortunately, the translator made no attempt to remedy the misunderstanding. All three monks walked out of the temple. They came back at intervals and made it known that they would return only under certain conditions. It was not Luang Phaw's position to bargain and he refused them audience. In the meantime he became ill.

By the time Kapilavaḍḍho returned to Thailand again in order to ask some sort of forgiveness, it was already too late, because Luang Phaw had already been overtaken by illness and was unable to receive guests. Luang Phaw's heart condition deteriorated — never to recover again — as if the dashing of his dreams for Dhamma to reach out to the world had at the same time destroyed his physical health. Kapilavaḍḍho returned to England in March 1956 to attend to his duties with the English Sangha Trust, and eventually he disrobed in England due to faltering health.

10
A Passing & A New Hope

"Place your mind at the centre of the Buddha inside — that's equivalent to touching upon the incalculable myriad of Buddhas (in Nirvana)."
(Phramonkolthepmuni)

It is evident from the teaching of Luang Phaw Wat Paknam that his wisdom and compassion were beyond measure. When the first signs of illness started to manifest themselves, Luang Phaw seemed anxious, not because his own life was coming to an end, but, as he later confided to close relatives, because he had no heir to the Dhammakāya Tradition. He was afraid the tradition would disappear soon after his death. One day in 1944 five relatives come to visit him and in spite of his illness, they detected a smile on Luang Phaw's face. When asked why Luang Phaw was smiling, he explained that he was relieved to say that the one who would perpetuate the Dhammakāya Tradition had just been born in Singburi province. He said that to find an heir to this tradition was the hardest thing in the world — but that heir had been born — his adeptness in meditation would be unrivalled and his power more potent than Luang Phaw's — sufficiently powerful to spread *Vijjā Dhammakāya* throughout the world.

Luang Phaw knew his disease was incurable. He took medicine only to postpone death. He said calmly:

> "This illness is the fruition of my past evil deeds — it is unavoidable. The medicine they give me doesn't cure the illness within. It's as if there is a huge, impermeable stone blocking the path of the medicine, stopping the medicine from being absorbed where it's really needed."

In 1956, Luang Phaw had been diagnosed as suffering from hypertension and as his monastic responsibilities grew more onerous, his chances for a full recovery dimmed. Luang Phaw planned to invite 2,500 monks to celebrate two and a half millenia of Buddhism in 1957,[1] but had to cancel the ceremony because of his waning health.

He was well aware of his situation but could not help himself. In spite of his physical suffering, he kept his mind strong, never complaining about pain or discomfort. The doctors could only find out whether he was in pain or not by asking him directly. He would always brush away those who tried to help him stand up or sit-down. He considered himself, for all purposes, a healthy person, unless he ran the risk of passing-out in public.

Although suffering, he would refuse to break off from his rains-retreat vows and take treatment outside the temple until the retreat was ended.

Besides hypertension, he suffered a hernia, necessitating surgery at Siriraj Hospital and the Monastic Hospital. When he finally agreed to enter hospital, he remained as strict as though he were in his own temple. One of the nurses came to attend to Luang Phaw on the first night. All the male nurses had gone home. As the nurse drew

---

1. Including the establishment of Thailand's most famous Buddhist parkland called Buddhamonthon, Nakorn Pathom from Newell *ibid*. p.99

close, Luang Phaw asked his attendant, Poong Mikaewnoi, who had come to tend him. When Luang Phaw found out that the nurse was female, he said,"That's all I want to know — take me back to my temple this minute!"

Luang Phaw would rather die, forgoing his operation than allow women to come into physical contact with him. Poong didn't know what to do. He called up Somdej Phra Wanarat and asked him to speak to the hospital manager. The Somdej did as he was bidden and made arrangements for male nurses around the clock.

By 1957 Luang Phaw's condition had worsened. He knew he would not live much longer and arranged his own mother's funeral in order to return his debt of gratitude to her for the last time.

Even when Luang Phaw was severely ill, his mind was still engrossed with Dhamma and meditation research. Every evening he would call the monks to meditate near him for one or two hours. At night he required everyone to meditate.

Even while ill, he never asked for special food or treatment. He ate whatever he was offered. He never rested from teaching meditation until the last day of his life. Before passing away, he chided his disciples saying:

> "Our reach is too short. We cannot beat Māra this lifetime. We are still in his clutches."

His words, however, were not meant as an insult to the meditation ability of his disciples. He didn't mean to accuse them of failure. He simply wanted to make sure they knew that the work was not finished so that no one should rest on their laurels until victory was achieved. Before Luang Phaw died, he made prophecies about the temple. He said that Wat Paknam would become very popular and there would be many new students coming to join the congregation. He ordered the nuns *not* to cremate his body but rather to embalm it. His corpse would continue to ensure the prosperity of the temple — 'nurturing' those who lived on by attracting pilgrims to visit Wat Paknam and pay homage. Instructions for meditation would be received from a tape recording of his voice in the chamber where his body lay. All these pilgrims would thus continue to make donations for the prosperity of the temple.

As Luang Phaw's health faltered, he no longer had the strength to train the newest workshop meditators or lead meditation sessions. One day Luang Phaw called Kuhn Yay Chandra and ordered:

> "Don't be in a hurry to die! Don't give up the teaching life for the seclusion of the forests! After my passing the others will have to rely on *you* to teach *Vijjā Dhammakāya* and keep them on the straight and narrow path. If you don't teach them, they will fall victim to the work of the Māra."

Without Luang Phaw's involvement, the emphasis of the temple tended to swing further and further in the direction of academic studies and the core of meditating adepts fled the temple to carry on their meditation elsewhere. Luang Phaw's last words were:

> "Carry on doing the work as if I were alive. Never stop meditating. Keep doing good and continue to support the monks."

Luang Phaw passed away on 3 February 1959 at the age of seventy-three.

Despite the majesty of a lifetime's ministry, when he passed away only a pitiful few of his disciples, principally the nuns who had stayed at his side throughout his ministry, continued with Luang Phaw's mission in its original spirit. Other followers tried to recapture the meditation experience they had attained with Luang Phaw by leaving the temple and retreating to the forests to meditate.

One day Kuhn Yay Chandra returned to her *kuti* to find a palmist sitting on her doorstep. "You will have a large number of students and will be a refuge to thousands of people," the palmist explained, offering his services for free. "You can't expect me to believe that!" said Kuhn Yay. "I live alone and I have nothing. I have no students. I have nothing but this small *kuti*."

As if in response to Luang Phaw's prophecy, a new generation of students interested in meditation started to come to Wat Paknam Bhasicharoen and sought out Kuhn Yay Upāsikā Chandra Kohn·nok·yoong at her humble kuti. Kuhn Yay didn't think much of it, but remembering Luang Phaw's words, she started to teach them to the best of her ability. She taught until the group outgrew both her *kuti* and the limited space in the compound of Wat Paknam. To overcome the limitations of space, at the age of sixty, she founded a new temple in Patum Thani province called 'Wat Phra Dhammakāya'.

*

Today Luang Phaw's personality is still a living force. It still remains a matter of wonder to many high-ranking ecclesiastics that Luang Phaw could exert such an influence on the minds of the faithful, even after his decease.

The great compassion of Luang Phaw Wat Paknam in teaching the profundities of *Vijjā Dhammakāya* to a core of disciples during his lifetime has turned out to be an undying achievement: like the ever widening ripples on the surface of a pond. Today, followers of Luang Phaw Wat Paknam number millions with students of Dhammakāya meditation throughout the world. More than ever, young students inspired by the tradition are curious about the life and example of the one who established the tradition of *Vijjā Dhammakāya*.

Epilogue

"Buddhism can only exist for as long as common people see the value of giving. If people were to stop giving food and sustenance, even for a single month, Buddhism would disappear from Thailand. All the monks and novices would have to disrobe."

(Phramonkolthepmuni)

The peoples' faith and support of Buddhism is in direct proportion to the devotion and discipline of the monastic community. The times of Luang Phaw Wat Paknam were times of great trial for the monastic community of Thailand. In many places, monks ordained only temporarily and did not uphold the faith of householders who expected teachings more profound than those that could be apprehended within only a few days of ordination. In the cities especially the monks devoted all of their energy to the study of texts but forgot that the real purpose of their scriptural studies was as a foundation for meditation.

The study of meditation before the time of Luang Phaw Wat Paknam was restricted to the forest monks and it was widely held that *arahant*s had disappeared from the world since the time of the Buddha; therefore it was useless to try to emulate the efforts of the saints of old. Even if any of the forest monks had achieved any attainments, the likelihood of passing the benefits of these teachings on to the general public was as remote as the forest temples themselves. Thus, except for the initiated few who had first-hand experience of ordination, the process of secularization of monastic study alienated the public from practising Buddhism. This accounts for the fact that many monks in Bangkok at the turn of the century were almost starving.

The most important discovery of Luang Phaw Wat Paknam was that historical Prince Siddhartha could only become enlightened as Lord Buddha through meditating until he attained the 'body of enlightenment' or '*Dhammakāya*' inside. By understanding the real essence of the Buddhist religion, he was able to teach the public how to give, to keep the Precepts and to meditate, so as to gain immediate benefits in their everyday lives — he taught them to bring their minds to a standstill at the centre of the body whatever merit they performed. Because Luang Phaw was always available to receive guests in the temple, despite his heavy commitments to internal training in the temple, the number of people to benefit from his teaching of Buddhism was very large indeed.

Luang Phaw was very open to new ideas. He pioneered the mass teaching of meditation made possible by the latest microphone technology. He gave sermons and taught to the general public by the hundreds. He also made tape recordings of his teachings for posterity.

Another pioneering breakthrough of Luang Phaw's was the introduction of an 'industrial revolution' in the teaching of meditation, his meditation workshop and its 'shift system' which allowed perpetual meditation around the clock, was truly innovative.

Luang Phaw Wat Paknam was instrumental in the construction of Thailand's biggest national Buddhist parkland and was the most successful of his generation in preserving elements of the oral tradition of meditation in Theravada Buddhism against the homogenizing influence of scripturally-based techniques of his time. He had a significant pioneering input to the nascent Sangha of Great Britain and is the pioneer of one of the Thai interpretations of meditation and Dhamma most visible beyond Thailand today. In spite of these contributions, Luang Phaw Wat Paknam ironically remains little recognized in academic writing.[1]

The depth of the teachings of *Vijjā Dhammakāya* discovered by Luang Phaw Wat Paknam is hard to express in words. *Vijjā Dhammakāya* can be equated with the Threefold Knowledge, Sixfold Higher Knowledge and the Eightfold Supra-normal Knowledge — the realms of knowledge of the *arahant*s in the time of Lord Buddha. The *arahants* from five-hundred years after the *parinirvana* of the Buddha up to the time in 1916 when Luang Phaw Wat Paknam rediscovered the *Dhammakāya,* were *arahants* putting an end to their defilements, but they had no further insight into the workings of the universe. It was this realm of supramundane knowledge which Luang Phaw Wat Paknam rediscovered and applied for the benefit of the world — but at the same time he himself never claimed himself to be an *arahant* or to have attained any of the stages of sainthood known in Buddhism. He didn't claim to be a Buddha or a *bodhisattva*.

The personality of Luang Phaw Wat Paknam continues to remain close to the hearts of all who practise meditation. His zeal for and commitment to meditation remain an undying legacy for us all.

---

1. from Newell *ibid*. pp..76, 99, 117, 270

Acknowledgments

This book could not have been written without the autobiographical notes of Luang Phaw Wat Paknam (Phramonkolthepmuni) together with the biographies written by the late Supreme Patriarch Ariyawongsakatañana (Bun Punnasiri Mahathera), Phra Thip Pariñña, Chao Kuhn Phrabhavanakosolthera (Vira Gunuttamo), and the verbal accounts from his close disciples such as H.E. Somdej Phramahārājamaṅgalacharn (Chuang Varapuñño) present abbot of Wat Paknam Bhasicharoen, Phrarajbhavanavisudh (Chaibul Dhammajayo) present abbot of Wat Phra Dhammakāya, Phrabhavanaviriyakuhn (Phadet Dattajeevo) present Vice-Abbot of Wat Phra Dhammakāya, Kuhn Yay Upāsikā Chandra Kohn·nok·yoong founder of Wat Phra Dhammakāya, Acharn Treeta Niemkam President of the Luang Phaw Wat Paknam Bhasicharoen Alumni Association, Kuhn Poong & Srinuan Mikaewnoi. Thanks also to Phra Nicholas Thanissaro for final translation and compilation of the manuscript, to Warangkana Tempati for her draft translations and to Manikanto Bhikkhu, Acharn Manit Ratanasuwan, Acharn Suwanee Srisopha and Aroonlak Jaiyanandana for their constructive criticism. Thanks to Robert Mawson and Chatchai Sribundith for revisions to the second and third editions and to Phra Terry Suratano and the team at *Triple-Gem.net* for corrections and magnanimous assistance in identifying sources in this fourth edition.

Bibliography

Bechert, H. (1966) *Buddhismus, Staat und Gesellschaft in den Länden des Theravāda, Part 3*, (Hamburg: Metzner)

Magness, T. (1964) *The Life and Teaching of the Venerable Chao Khun Mongkol-Thepmuni, the late abbot of Wat Paknam Bhasicharoen* (Bangkok: Groarke)

Newell, C.S. (2008) *Monks, meditation and missing links: continuity, "orthodoxy" and the vijjā dhammakāya in Thai Buddhism,* PhD. Diss. (SOAS, Univ. of London).

Tansomboon, A. (2004) *An Analysis of the Phra Mongkol Thepmuni's (Sodh Candasaro) Buddha Dhamma Propagation,* MA. Diss. (Mahachulalongkorn Rajavidyalaya Univ., Bangkok)

Glossary

Anusāvanācāriya — the junior examining monk of the two monastic examiners at the ordination whose duty is to give teachings and advice to the ordinand.

Arahant — one who has purified themselves of all defilements, and who, on death of the physical body will attain Nirvana. He has escaped *Samsara* and will not be reborn.

Bhikkhu — a Buddhist monk

Bodhisattva — an aspirant for Buddhahood (in Theravāda Buddhism) or one who holds the vow not to enter upon Nirvana until they have helped all living beings to attain enlightenment (in Mahāyāna Buddhism).

Buddha — the enlightened one, historical founder of the Buddhist religion.

Dhamma — the Teachings of the Lord Buddha (if capitalized) or things arising in the mind (if not capitalized).

Dhammakāya — the body of enlightenment or Buddha Nature.

Dhammayuttikā — the name of a reformed Buddhist sect founded by H.M. King Rama IV (Maha Mongkut)

Discipline, monastic — the 227 rules of conduct that govern the daily life of a monk as described in the Buddhist book of Discipline (Vinaya).

Eightfold Supranormal Knowledge — the mental powers of one pure of defilements, comprising: 1. insight knowledge; 2. mind-made magical power; 3. supernormal powers; 4. divine ear; 5. reading the minds of others; 6. recollection of past lives; 7. divine eye, and; 8. the knowledge of an end of defilements.

Kammavācācāriya — the senior examining monk of the two monastic examiners at the ordination whose duty it is to report before the monastic assembly the presence or absence of circumstances obstructing the candidate's ordination.

Karma — the Buddhist law of retribution that one who does good deeds will receive good rewards, one who does evil deeds will receive evil retribution. Sometimes used to refer to the retributive effects of past deeds.

Kaṭhina — the major Buddhist ceremony of robes-offering held to mark the end of the Rains Retreat

Kuṭi — hut or simple cottage used by a monk as accommodation

Mahānikāya — the orthodox remainder of the Thai community left unreformed after the formation of the Dhammayuttikā Sect.

Mahāyāna — the reformed school of Buddhism found in the Far East which is based on Scriptures written in Sanskrit or Chinese.

Mantra — a word or formula repeated silently during meditation to assist concentration of mind

Māra — the personification of evil forces in the world which delude the unwitting into contentment with life in *Samsara*. Can be escaped and defeated only by the practice of meditation.

Nirvana — the ultimate goal of Buddhist endeavour — Ultimate Bliss, Eternity and True Self, release from defilements and Samsara.

Pali — the ancient Indian language used to record the scriptures of the Theravāda Buddhist school.

Paṭhama magga — the trailhead of the Path to Nirvana manifesting inwardly to meditators as a diamond-clear sphere, when the mind comes to a standstill. Can be equated with the first absorption [*jhāna*].

Pāṭimokkha — the summary of the monastic Precepts and rules in the Vinaya recited twice a month in every monastery.

Precepts — Buddhist rules of training governing conduct and speech.

Quarter-moon days — the full-moon, half-moon and new-moon days of the lunar calendar, traditionally the days for special activities in Buddhist temples.

Rains Retreat — the period of three months during the monsoon when monks traditionally limit travel outside the temple and focus instead on meditation activities.

Requisites, monastic — a monk's eight basic possessions: three robes, a belt, a bowl, a razor, a needle and a water filter.

Samanera — a Buddhist novice monk, usually under the age of twenty, who holds Ten Precepts.

Samatha — the initial practice of meditation that leads the mind to come to a standstill. c.f. **Vipassanā**

Samsara — the cycle of birth, sickness, death and rebirth which ensnares those unable to renounce sensual pleasure — escapable only through meditation until the mind reaches a standstill.

Saṅgha — the monastic community or Order

Sāsana — the Buddhist Teaching or Buddhist religion

Sixfold Superknowledge — the mental powers of one pure of defilements comprising: 1. supernormal powers; 2. divine ear; 3. reading the minds of others; 4. recollection of past lives; 5. divine eye, and; 6. the knowledge of an end of defilements.

Theravāda — the orthodox school of Buddhism found in Southeast Asia and Sri Lanka which is based on Scriptures written in Pali.

Threefold Knowledge — the mental powers of one pure of defilements, comprising: 1. recollection of past lives; 2. knowledge of the decease and rebirth of beings, and; 3. the knowledge of an end of defilements.

Triple Gem — the highest refuge of Buddhism — Buddha, Dhamma and Sangha — which can be discovered within by those who meditate.

Vassa — see **Rains Retreat**

Vijjā Dhammakāya — the Dhammakāya Tradition, or the wisdom gained by those practicing Vipassanā meditation beyond the attainment of *Dhammakāya*. Can be equated with Threefold Knowledge, Sixfold Superknowledge and Eightfold Supranormal Knowledge.

Vinaya — see **Discipline, monastic**

Vipassana — the practice of meditation beyond attainment of the still mind that leads the mind to insight. c.f. **Samatha**

Index

How to Meditate

Meditation is a state of ease, inner peace and happiness that we can bring into being, ourselves. It is a practice recommended by Buddhism for happiness, non-recklessness, mindfulness and wisdom in everyday life. It is no mystery, but something which can be easily practised by all following the technique taught by Phramonkolthepmuni (Sodh Candasaro), Luang Phaw Wat Paknam as follows:

Step-by-Step Instructions for the Meditation Technique

(1) Paying respect to the Triple Gem: To start one should soften one's mind by paying respect to the Triple Gem, before taking Five or Eight Precepts to consolidate one's virtue;

(2) Recollect your goodness: Kneel or sit with your feet to one side and think of all the good deeds you have done throughout the day, from your past, and all the good deeds you intend to do in the future. Recollect such good deeds in such a way, until you feel as if your whole body seems to be filled with tiny particles of goodness;

(3) Sit for meditation, relaxing body and mind: Sit in the half-lotus position, upright with your back and spine straight - cross-legged with your right leg over the left one. Your hands should rest palms-up on your lap, and the tip of your right index finger should touch your left thumb. Try to find a position of poise for yourself. Don't take up a position where you have to force or stress yourself unnaturally - but at the same time, don't slouch! Softly close your eyes as if you were falling asleep. Don't squeeze your eyes shut and make sure you have no tension across your eyebrows. Relax every part of your body, beginning with the muscles of your face, then relax your face, neck shoulders, arms, chest, trunk and legs. Make sure there are no signs of tension on your forehead or across your shoulders. Focus on the task in hand, creating a feeling of ease in your mind. Feel that the you are entering upon a supreme state of calm and ease with both body and mind.

(4) Imagine a crystal ball as the object of your meditation: Imagine a clear, bright, flawless crystal ball as if it is floating at the centre of your body (*see seventh base of the mind in the illustration*). The crystal ball should be pure and soothing, like twinkling starlight to the eye. At the same time, softly repeat the sound of the mantra '*Sammā-Arahaṃ*' to yourself as 'recollection of the Buddha' over and over again. Alternatively you can start by imagining the crystal ball at the first base of the mind, and gradually move it down to the seventh base via the other six bases (*see diagram*) while repeating the mantra to yourself.

*

Once the crystal ball becomes visible at the centre of the body, continue to maintain a feeling of ease, as if the mental object seen is part of that feeling. If the crystal ball should disappear, don't feel disappointed - just keep the same feeling of ease in your mind as before, and imagine a new crystal ball in place of the old. If the mental object should appear anywhere else other than the centre of the body, gradually lead the object to the centre of the body, without using even the slightest of force. When the mental object has come to a standstill at the centre of the body, place the attention at the centre of that object, by imagining that there is an additional tiny star visible

THE SEVEN BASES OF THE MIND

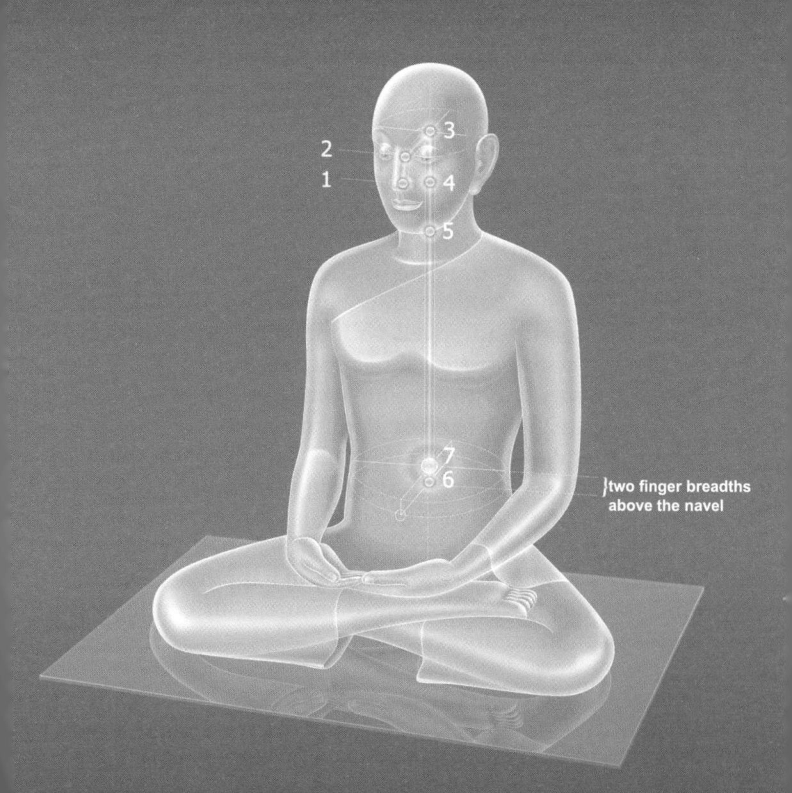

there. Focus your mind continuously on the tiny star at the centre of the object of meditation. The mind will adjust itself until it comes to a perfect standstill. At that point, the mind will fall through the centre and there will be a new brighter sphere which arises in place of the original one. This new sphere is known as the 'Pa.thama-magga sphere' or 'sphere of Dhamma'. This sphere is the gateway or trailhead to the pathway to Nirvana.

Imagining the object of meditation is something you can do the whole of the time, wherever you may be, whether sitting, standing, walking, lying-down or performing other activities.

It is advised to imagine in such a way continuously at every moment of the day - but imagining without force. No matter how well you manage, you should be contented with your level of progress, in order to prevent excessive craving for immediate results becoming a hindrance to your progress. If you meditate until having attained a steadfast, diamond-bright 'sphere of Dhamma' at the centre of your body, you should try to maintain it by recollecting it as continuously as you can.

In such a way, the benefits of your meditation will not only keep your life on the pathway of happiness, success and non-recklessness, but also ensure your continuing progress in meditation.

ADDITIONAL ADVICE

1. *Avoid force:* Never force anything in your meditation. Don't squeeze your eyes closed thinking you will see the object of meditation more quickly. Don't tense your arms, your abdomen or your body - because any form of tension will only cause the mind to be displaced from the centre of the body to the place you are tensing.

2. ***Don't crave after seeing something:*** You should always maintain complete neutrality of mind. Don't let your mind be distracted from the object of meditation and the mantra. Don't worry yourself about when the object of meditation will appear. The image will appear itself when it comes to the right time, just as the sun rises and sets in its own time.
3. ***Don't worry about your breath:*** Meditating in this technique starts with the visualization of a bright object [*āloka kasiṇa*]. Once having meditated until attaining the sphere of Dhamma, one continues with meditation by passing through the refined human body (astral body), the angelic body, the form-Brahma body and the formless-Brahma body until attaining the Dhamma body (or *Dhammakāya*). Only then is one equipped to turn one's meditation towards insight [*vipassanā*]. Thus there is no need to practise mindfulness of the breath at any stage.
4. ***Maintain your mind at the centre of the body all the time:*** Even after having finished your formal sitting, maintain your mind at the centre of the body the whole of the time. No matter whether you are standing, walking, sitting or lying-down, don't allow your mind to slip away from the centre of the body. Continue repeating the mantra '*Sammā-Arahaṃ*' to yourself while visualizing the crystal ball at the centre of the body.
5. ***Bring all objects arising in the mind to the centre of the body:*** No matter what appears in the mind, bring it (gently) to the centre of the body. If the object disappears, there is no need to chase around looking for it. Just continue to rest your attention at the centre of the body while repeating the mantra to yourself. Eventually, when the mind becomes yet more peaceful, a new object of meditation will appear.

The basic meditation described here will lead to a deepening of happiness in life. If one doesn't abandon the practice but cultivates meditation regularly, to the point that the sphere of Dhamma is attained, one should try to maintain that sphere at the centre of one's body for the remainder of one's life, while leading one's life in a scrupulous way. It will offer one a refuge in life and will bring happiness both in this lifetime and the hereafter.

SUMMARY OF THE BENEFITS OF MEDITATION

1. Personal Benefits for the meditator

- *The Mind:* the mind will feel at ease - calm and peaceful. Memory will also improve;
- ***Personality:*** self-confidence will be improved. The true nature of calm will become apparent. Anger will diminish, leaving only the feeling of kindness towards others;
- ***Daily life:*** will be increased in quality in the new-found absence of stress. The results of work or study will be much more successful. The meditator can enjoy health of both body and mind;
- ***Ethics and decision-making:*** a right understanding of that which is good and that which is bad, will be clearly seen for any given situation. Important decisions will cause less worry because the meditator understands the outcome of his actions. The meditator can refrain from harmful actions and decisions, instead being content and confident about choices made.

2. Benefits for the Meditator's Family

- ***Peace and success:*** family life will be more harmonious, through the increased mutual respect and consideration between family members. Parents will be better able to lead the family successfully;

- *Cooperation:* Family members will be more enthusiastic to honour their duties and co-operate towards solving shared problems.

3. National Benefits

- *Peaceful Society:* most grave social problems originate from unwholesomeness of mind. If everybody learns to meditate and live peacefully, 'endemic' problems like crime and drug abuse will be diminished;
- *Respect:* Respect for others will be improved simply through keeping to a routine of meditation and following moral precepts. Honesty will diminish suspicion in the community;
- *A caring society:* as a result of meditation, the peacefulness of life can be more widely enjoyed and there will be a more widespread willingness to participate in social work

4. Spiritual Benefits

- *Understanding eternity:* all people, with or without their own faith can deepen the understanding of their own spirituality through meditation. Meditators of all faiths, through the practice of meditation, can explore their own faith in depth, particularly with reference to the understanding of eternity in their chosen faith;
- *Inspiration:* inspiration in your own spiritual tradition is strengthened as the meditator comes to realize the profound happiness that can be found through meditation;
- *Prolonging the lifetime of spiritual traditions:* the meditator's own spiritual tradition will be maintained as newcomers have a better understanding of moral conduct and self-discipline.

Follow-up Contacts

International Branches: There are more than fifty Dhammakaya meditation centres worldwide which offer a selection of activities on Buddhism and meditation in Thai and local languages. An up-to-date list of contacts can be found at:

www.dhammakaya.net/en/centers/center-continent

World Peace Ethics Contest: A multi-lingual yearly contest to test knowledge of Buddhist ethics as they relate to the family is organized at Dhammakaya branches worldwide:

www.vir2kidz.com

Dhammakaya Meditation Retreats: Meditation retreats following the Dhammakaya Tradition can be booked with the Middle Way meditation retreats in Thailand and on tour abroad:

www.meditationthai.org

Temporary Ordination: An international ordination scheme is held each July at the main Dhammakaya Temple in Thailand in English and Mandarin:

www.ordinationthai.org

Distance Learning: By distance learning it is possible to study Buddhism and meditation at degree level via Dhammakaya's Open University:

www.dou.us

Peace Revolution: meditation mentoring and activities in Thailand for an online community of young people in non-religious context can be found at:

www.peacerevolution2010.org

Luang Phaw Wat
Paknam Bhasicharoen
Phramonkolthepmuni
(Sodh Candasaro)
(1885-1959)
the rediscoverer of
the Dhammakaya
tradition of medita-
tion lost to the world
for over two-thousand
years.

Above: Wat (Boatbon) Bangkuvieng, Nonthaburi, where Luang Phaw Wat Paknam rediscovered the Dhammakaya tradition in 1914.

Right: Wat Bangpla, Banglain, Nakorn Pathom, where Luang Phaw gave his first teaching on Dhammakaya and where his first disciple was to attain Dhammakaya in Luang Phaw's footsteps.

Above: inside the chapel of Wat (Boatbon) Bangkuvieng, Nonthaburi, the place that Luang Phaw Wat Paknam staked his life in meditation to attain the Dhammakaya and recover the wisdom known to the Buddha.

Above: Luang Phaw teaching the 'bases of the mind' — the basics of meditation in the Dhammakaya tradition, for the general public.

Below: 'May any monk still to come, come quickly to join this temple. May any monk already here stay all of his life.' The monastic community of Wat Paknam under Luang Phaw's guidance.

Above: Luang Phaw Wat Paknam presenting Triple Robes to Novice William Purfurst (alias Richard Randall) at the latter's full ordination as 'Kapilavaddho Bhikkhu' on Visakha Puja Day 1954.

Below: Wat Paknam Bhasicharoen, Thonburi, in the present day, one of the leading Buddhist centres in Thailand.

Luang Phaw receiving guests and distributing souvenir amulets.

Right: Kuhn Yay Maharatana Upasika Chandra Kohn-nok-yoong (1909-2000) the leading disciple of Luang Phaw Wat Paknam and founder of Wat Phra Dhammakaya who (below) perpetuated the Dhammakaya tradition during the sixties until over-crowding necessitated expansion at a new site in Patumthani province called 'Wat Phra Dhammakaya' in 1970.

H.E. Somdej Phramaharajamangalacharn (Chuang Varapuñño) [centre], Ven. Master Hsing Yun [right centre] and Phrabhavanaviriyakhun (Phadet Dattajeevo) [right] pour molten gold to cast the image of Luang Phaw Wat Paknam at the World Dhammakaya Centre (WDC.), Wat Phra Dhammakaya, Patumthani province, Thailand on 25 February 1994.